The Gasconade Review Presents:
Wolf at the Door / Nobody Home

Edited by John Dorsey and Jason Ryberg

Spartan Press

OAC BOOKS
OSAGE ARTS COMMUNITY

Spartan Press
Kansas City, MO
spartanpresskc@gmail.com

OAC Books
Belle, MO
www.osageac.org

Spartan
Press

OAC
BOOKS
OSAGE ARTS COMMUNITY

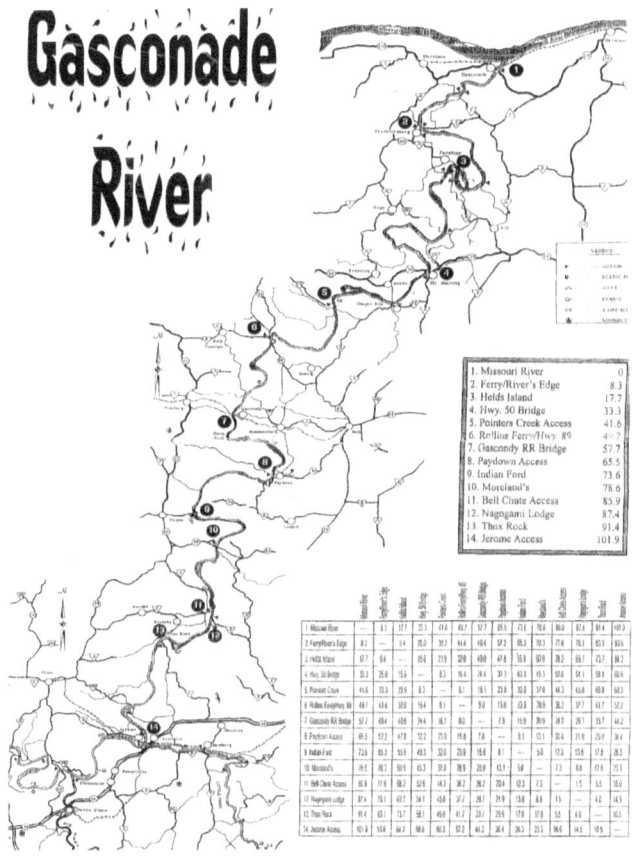

Gasconade River

		Mileage
1. Missouri River	0	
2. Ferry/River's Edge	8.3	
3. Helds Island	17.7	
4. Hwy. 50 Bridge	33.3	
5. Pointers Creek Access	41.6	
6. Rollins Ferry/Hwy 89	49.7	
7. Gasconady RR Bridge	57.7	
8. Paydown Access	65.5	
9. Indian Ford	73.6	
10. Moreland's	78.6	
11. Bell Chute Access	85.9	
12. Nagogami Lodge	87.4	
13. Thox Rock	91.4	
14. Jerome Access	101.9	

The **Gasconade River** is about 280 miles (450 km) long and is located in central and south-central Missouri in the United States. The Gasconade River begins in the Ozarks southeast of Hartville in Wright County and flows generally north-north-eastwardly through Wright, Laclede, Pulaski, Phelps, Maries, Osage and Gasconade counties, through portions of the Mark Twain National Forest. It flows into the Missouri River near the town of Gasconade in Gasconade County.

The name Gasconade is derived from "Gascon", an inhabitant of the French region of Gascony. The people of that province were noted for their boastfulness. It was applied by the early French to the Indians living on its banks who bragged about their exploits. The name means to boast or brag, and thus the river received its name. The waters of the river are boisterous and boastful and the name is also descriptive.

The headwaters of the Gasconade are in the southeastern corner of Webster County northeast of Seymour, Missouri where it drains the eastern margin of the Springfield Plateau at approximately 37°11'54"N 92°41'44"W. The river joins the Missouri River at the city of Gasconade at 38°40'28"N 91°32'55"W The river follows a meandering course through the Ordovician age dolostone and sandstone bedrock of the Ozark Salem Plateau creating spectacular bluffs and incised meanders along the way. Numerous springs and caves occur within the drainage area and along the river course. Significant tributaries include the Osage Fork of Webster and Laclede counties and Roubidoux Creek and Big Piney River of Texas and Pulaski counties. The Roubidoux and Big Piney flow respectively along the west and east boundaries of Fort Leonard Wood which lies a short distance south and east of the Gasconade.

The plateau surface near the midpoint is 300 feet (91 metres) above the river bottom near the river midpoint northeast of Waynesville creating scenic river bluffs. At the junction with the Missouri the river bottom is about 400 feet (120 m) lower in elevation than the old plateau surface above the river. The elevation of the plateau rim at the headwaters is at or above 1,600 feet (490 m) with local hilltops at over 1,700 feet (520 m) (second highest elevation in Missouri near Cedar Gap). The elevation at the confluence with the Missouri is 500 feet (150 m) giving an overall drainage basin relief of 1,200 feet (370 m).

It is ranked with a difficulty of I and II (seldom) by those who canoe, kayak and float. It is considered a good float stream because there's typically not a heavy congestion of boats. It is common to go for many miles without seeing another boat.

There are caves and an abundance of wildlife along the river and is considered a popular place by anglers for its largemouth bass and smallmouth bass.

The Gasconade River is the longest river completely within the boundary of Missouri. It has been called one of the world's crookedest rivers.

The *Gasconade Review* is a literary and arts publication based out of the Osage Arts Community (http://osageac.org/), located on the Gasconade River, just outside of Belle, Missouri. It appears twice annually, focusing primarily, but not exclusively, on writers and artists from the region and state, but occasionally also features *folks what ain't from around here*. All submissions must be hand delivered between the months of April and October and the hours of 3pm to 6pm. A decent bourbon is appreciated. Proper river attire required. Don't worry, the dogs won't bite.

TABLE OF CONTENTS

Image 2 / *Ballpoint pen, 12x18 cms, 11-5-21*, by Normon J. Olson

Ballpoint pen, 12x18 cms, 11-5-21, by Normon J. Olson

KEN GIERKE

My Paddle Slices the Water

And my mind shifts gears,
one heartbeat waiting for the next
as the scene unfolds, frame by frame.
The paddle moves in a slow arc behind,
beside, before me. Drops of water stretch,
fall along the same path, the paddle
already nearing the top of its arc
even as it enters the water, one stroke
a delayed mirror of the other, both
occurring in a breath that spans seconds.

A kingfisher weaves past me as I count
each beat of its wings, hear its trill
in one long note in odd harmony
with the slush of water leaving the paddle
beside me. A turtle dives from a tree
emerging from the river, its shell
half-submerged and surrounded by a crown,
water creeping skyward to accept it.
Fish in mouth, a heron rises from the bank,
the rhythm of its wings nearly at a standstill.

My mind shifts gears once more,
one heartbeat follows another,
the heron recedes, the turtle disappears,
and the kingfisher is lost to sight.

My paddle slices the water.

The Final Cost

A river course that bears the name
of those who once lived here
bears likeness, none,
to anyone
of those who once lived here.

For tribes long gone will not appear.
Their time here was undone.
When double-crossed,
the Osage lost.
Their time here was undone.

To take their land a tale was spun,
their home the final cost.
Yes, all should know
the fatal blow,
their home the final cost.

This stream they once were known to cross
goes on without their grace.
The white man's claim,
a nation's shame,
goes on without their grace.

The people who were once erased
will never be the same.
The land held dear
in yesteryear
will never be the same.

Downstream

Paddle slices the surface,
kayak glides, my wake
the only waves visible.

Cardinal calls. Turtles bask
in morning sun. Eagle lands
in towering sycamore.

Heron recedes downstream,
it's wings stately
in their slow steady beat.

Rising. Falling.
Subject to season.
Wings and water, as one.

Always, it flows,
meandering, as life will do.
River holds all, and more.

JONATHAN S. BAKER

Hyacinths

All these years later
I can finally say it
wasn't your scent
that drove me
to a place of bliss
but the fragrance
of hyacinths
carried on the wind
that rainy afternoon
in Boonville.
Hyacinths like those that grew
by the front porch
of my home and I picked
for my mother
and it makes me smile
to think about now.
You aren't the monster
I remember.
I was foolish
for fearing you,
but also unwise
for ever loving you.

Holy Rolling, Batman!

It's 1966,
a friend
gives you
something
and tells you,
"just take it.
It'll be fun."
An hour passes
and you see
some fem kid
in a gold cape
sitting alone
in a black
convertible
tricked out
with fins.
Inside
the
What-a-Way
to
Go-Go,
an old queen
with cat ears
cape and mask
is downing
orange juice
and dances
til he falls
to the floor.
You ask yourself,
"Is Gotham bad
or is it this trip?"

Home Defense

Between two towns
where nothing happens
sat a house filled
with car parts and newspapers.
Bob lived inside
wearing coveralls
and a matted fur coat
reliving a war that broke him.
Airplanes would fly real low
to get a rise out of Bob.
One day a crop duster
buzzed Bob's old house
threading the space
between the roof
and the power lines.
Bob grabbed his rifle
and POW!
He got the plane
and nicked the pilot's thigh
Good ol' Bob,
fuckin' got that flyboy.

JEFF ALFIER

Eulogy for the Atchafalaya River

Through the brittle frame of an aged polaroid,
the flash of a red moon, I dreamt a mare

waded neck-high through nightfallen waters,
her mane flayed like a wing nailed to a wall.

She spanned that floodtide dead easy,
like a jubilant bride I once watched

through penumbras of stormlight,
dance solo in the rain.

I woke, and outside my window
between the spaces of my breathing,

saw my daughter sleepwalking
through lanterns of fireflies.

Catahoula Parish Transcendence

The closing chapter of the day is my lover
cleaning her shotgun, light's finale

in an unsettled breeze that offers nothing
but a ruse of rain, the screen door latched,

a sweater pulled over my father's shoulders,
a cottonmouth making one last glide

across Bayou Cocodrie to a watermark the moon
will unveil as stars hover farmland's

turned earth and waterfowl domains, nighthawks
summoning their dark hymns, and our daughter,

dropping a storybook to the floor, turns her face
toward sparrows fluttering in the attic.

Picture of My Mother Over a Winter Holiday

She slumbers on the family room couch,
wakens for a few spells to catch the MASH reruns,

then drifts again to a wider sleep. Sleet blusters
the sliding glass door behind her

before retreating
into the hazy silence of the gray sky.

Early evenings are the most demanding for her.
They seem to stretch beyond the clock's patience,

my father somewhere beyond her voice —
outside in his coal shed, or swearing

at some defiant gadget in the garage.
In the backyard, his chestnut trees

thrum to the slow dance of the wind.
He stays outside, scraping ice from the kitchen window.

KEVIN RIDGEWAY

My First Girlfriend

Had blonde dreadlocks
and a high pitched
make out voice.
She left me for
a guitar player
who strummed her
sweet dormitory heart
away from me,
which broke my silence
but not my angry young heart
as I shouted words that
made her never talk to me
again. She cut off her
dreadlocks when she left
the guitar player for a guy
too good for us both, and
I thought good for her.

Before Anyone Ever Really Knew Me

My friends in college and I would pass the joint
around and watch the video of my 10th birthday.

it was like they all grew up with me
and knew all the in jokes and what was going on
in my family at the time after I clued them in.

they laughed at the miniature me and my antics
with my only friend in attendance at the party.

they all left me there in front of the tv screen
blinded by a past that made it hard for me
to enjoy the present when they were my friends.

luckily when my college sweetheart divorced me,
she took that old tape and hid it in her mother's
basement alongside naked photos of me that will
expose me to several more generations to come
who will all feel kind of like they really knew me.

Andrew Dice Clay

made my mother laugh
a sleazy trickster wordplayerhater
decked out like a secondhand Elvis
ready to pull into our driveway
with Joey Buttofuco warming up
the front passenger seat
of a convertible for her
as they all rode in
tabloid daydreams
of defective guys
she could
never change.

TOHM BAKELAS

lifeburn

living alone
in a square room
with green walls
and a white ceiling,

having little money to eat
only ever enough to drink,

strung out on recurring thoughts
starving on screaming silence

at night the bed was magic,
the final platform
for the madness hours
to unwind and quiet down

and in those mornings
that always followed
lying in the bed
with the sheets pulled up
was all that was needed

and in rolling over
to escape the sun,
the bed balanced the body
as the mind tried
balancing the hangover
and the world.

springtime in denville

out by the gully
we tossed dreams for
quarters and conformity—
i still walk the water bank
following fox prints and feathers,
wading through broken memories
of lost love and dead friends.

i chase skybirds along
invisible migratory lines
and sift through silt of
conscious thoughts
and cracked teeth

ghosts fuck with my senses
and i feel all their love in me

my home town burns on
as the creeks run dry

it is 5:12 in the evening
and i'm drunk in the sun

tuesday, february 22, 2022

february rain hits the windshield
like gunfire i cannot avoid,
i'm driving to the post office
out of malformed habit

i park the car and the rain subsides

on the sidewalk
a broken pen rests,
a useless instrument
amongst rock salt and
cigarette butts

inside, the building is empty,
a spider watches my movements
and i leave with nothing

back outside on the sidewalk,
i stare at the broken pen

for a few seconds i forget
about what i need to do
and where i need to be

then the rain starts again,
and i am alone.

Rain Dance

"Hear that?" She turned toward the window.
"That's thunder!" She pulled back the curtain.
"The sky is cracking!" She looked at me.
I must have been acting gloomy because I couldn't play outside.

"Come on! Let's go see!" I started to tie my shoes.
"You don't need those! Let's go!"
She took my hand and pushed past the screen door.
Just in time rain began to fall from the grey sky.

Barefoot we ran across the lawn. We ran into the hayfield.
The rain was warm. Lightning shot gold in the distance.
She spread her arms and spun around. I did the same.
Her wide smile was drenched. Her long black hair was dripping.

She laughed for joy. I jumped up and down and laughed too.
She taught me summer rain was our friend, and that
how we felt had more to do with what was inside us,
rather than what was happening in the world on the outside.

She was up, she was down, but this is when I loved her best:
arms outstretched with the electricity branching behind her.
This is when I wasn't afraid of anything.
I was six years old, and she was my mother.

Scarecrow Joe

Joe ---- could be seen around town on his paper route or collecting cans. His tongue would be sticking out sideways, and his eyes swimming around. In a town full of dopey characters, Joe was something else. He was in his early twenties, but he played with sticks and rolled down grassy hills.

Once my little metal-head friends and I were mucking around on our bikes looking for a place to smoke weed when Joe ----- chased us down. He turned slightly, put his hand to his mouth, and make a static noise like he was on a walkie-talkie. Then he said, "Those are my men. They're coming for you guys!"

"Shut-up, Joe!"

"Yeah, get the fuck out of here Joe!"

One day I was driving with my dad and we passed Joe as he was talking to a Christmas tree that was left on the curb. "There's Joe -----," I said.

"Joe -----?" asked my dad. "That boy's still alive?"

"Yeah, he's something like the village idiot."

But my dad didn't laugh. And my dad loves to laugh. Instead he got serious. "I worked with his father, Brett ----, at the steel yard. This was before you were born. I was at the bar when Brett came in. He had just had a baby so we were surprised to see him out. He was crying and shaking. He couldn't put two words together. Finally, after a few stiff shots of rye Brett explained. He had hired a babysitter for his baby Joe while he was working the night shift. Apparently Joe wouldn't stop crying. So the babysitter put the little baby in the microwave and turned it on."

I told my friends not to swear at Joe anymore, even if he was annoying.

Wood Glue

Growing up in Wisconsin our beds had these big wooden headboards.
When I was eight or nine, my mother called me into my room.

"What are all these nicks in the headboard?!" I looked. There were tiny
dents on the top of the headboard. As far as I could remember they had
always been there.

She said, "I'll tell you what they are. I tested it. Yes, I did! I asked myself
what in this room could make this mark? So I picked up the alarm clock
and struck it against the wood. Sure enough, it made the EXACT mark!"

As if I didn't understand she began to demonstrate. She picked up the
alarm clock and began drumming the corner of it against the wood. It
made the rat-a-tat sound like a machinegun. When she was done the
alarm clock was scrambled.

"Is this what you do in here for fun?!" I shook my head no. "Well, this
is what is going to happen mister! I went to Ace Hardware. Yes I did! I
found this new product called wood glue." In the corner of my room was
a tub that said: Wood Glue. "What you are going to do is use this stuff to
fill in the dents of our nice wood headboard!"

She cracked the tub open, and handed me a large stick like an oversized
popsicle stick. "Here mister. What you do is take this stick and smear the
wood glue across the nicks and fill them in." She left the room.

So, holding back the tears I began. I scooped up some of the stuff and
ran it across the wood. It was white and pasty. It smeared. It got into the
dents alright, but now they looked like little zits. I didn't have
the words to argue with her, but I knew this was insane.

I tried to be tough, as boys are supposed to be, but the tears began to fall. Not just because I was innocent of making the dents. But because my mom seemed to think that this glue would go into these nicks and somehow magically turn into wood.

So I smeared and smeared until the headboard was worse than when I began. I knew that when she came back and saw this she would get angrier. I smeared the stuff hoping that my dad would come home in time. Then he would tell her that wood glue attached two pieces of wood together. It did not turn into wood.

KUSHAL PODDAR

Orgasms

I

The summer crawls over the hills
one noontime. Our shutters down,
on the sunless bed your revirginated
sea swells and ebbs.
My nose and mouth feel like flypapers
with all your sour and salt water.

I crave to desire summer, welcome it,
but our town at the foot of the hills
takes the worst whipping,
stays a bondage of the heat
until we writhe to recall the safe-word.
Sometimes it is 'Lemonade',
and often, 'Kiss'.

II

The summer laundry pays homage
to the martyred water,
salutes your taut red underwear
on the clothesline.

The zephyr stirs the pennon.
Two doves coo in our dust wrapped yard
as we make love somewhere inside.

Inside.

There exists a place where invasion
has no victim, and the consent negotiates
through our irises, and when we collapse
as ruins we erect good memories for the history.

My manhood coos now, a tired peace-bird.
You free it inside the cage formed with your fingers.

During The Wartime

I

Two models chunter on
bowel movement during the dieting
before an assignment.

The cafe is filled with
some hidden crumbs,
but no fly, none at all.

They have buzzed into
the territory outside this,
where the bodies keep
the slaughterhouses full,
and where the stomachs are empty.

II

Two old men finger-script silence
on each other's skin.
Those are their wartime memoirs -
of flashes and fire,
of forbidden love and affairs.

Their pet cock and its hens
peck around in the gloaming's garden.

The man does not have much to write.
'Hush' - they scriven again and again
until the skin gives way to the flesh,
and the alphabet tower tall like
buildings deserted and still unhurt
midst an erased landscape.

Peace Blooms

Peace blooms a complex flower;
its petals rivulet in this light;
I shiver in its impossible implosion.
Something I lost becomes
almost a grief, albeit not quite.

Not quite a whispering, and yet
when you propose availing
the blossom, say, "Let's use the peacetime,
piece together the pieces our bodies are."
my ears giggle at your bad pun.

The flower, if I play 'love/love-me-not' with,
yields a set of inconclusive results as if
we shall never know any better.

Ice Cubes

Friends are ice cubes in the cocktail of life.
We chill together, tinkle and clink our way

out of the shaker and into the glass, mix
with sass and effervescence, irreverence

and unabashed joy; we entertain one long-
pour, united in spirit, no matter the garnish.

Crush us, we stay frosty; swizzle-stir us, we
go with the flow. We get juicy; we get saucy —

we get what it means to melt together as
we age, diluting the bad times, enhancing

the good times, just enough bump and
tumble to let them know we were here.

Friends are ice cubes in the cocktail of life.
This is our celebration. This is our Happy Hour.

What You Need

— *after Aretha Franklin's "Respect"*

What you need, do you know I got it?
1967, a small white transistor radio.

It's the Summer of Love, baby, but
Detroit burns, Ginsberg chants to levitate
the Pentagon, Joan Baez blocks the entrance
to Oakland's Armed Services Induction Center,
John McCain is shot down and becomes a
P.O.W. Protests against the war in Vietnam
surge; troops engage in the Mekong Delta.
All they're askin' is for a little respect
when they come home.

Far out, man, Hair opens off-Broadway,
Hendrix wants to know if you've ever
been Experienced, Morrison is getting
high(er). Sock it to me, Sock it to me,
Sock it to me, Sock it to me....
The Queen of Soul climbs the charts.

What you want, baby I got it.
Martin Luther King is jailed for peaceful
protest, Carl Stokes is elected mayor
of Cleveland, President Lyndon B. Johnson
appoints Thurgood Marshall as Supreme
Court Justice. Take care, T. C. B.

The Freedom of Information Act
becomes effective, the Outer Space Treaty
is signed. It's a Human Be-In, a magical
mystery tour through a Cold War,
a Space Race, the Motown Sound at CKLW
coming to you out of Windsor-Detroit.

It's the 60s, baby, a transistor radio,
a twelve-year old girl listening to a Queen.
Find out what it means to me.
Aretha, nothing but R-E-S-P-E-C-T.

Heat

he turns up the heat

she turns down the heat
caught in the middle

blankets folded back, waiting
for the slide in of cold feet
the snuggle, the settle, sleep

M.J. ARCANGELINI

Echolalia In Practice

In the early 70s, when my grandmother was
briefly in a convalescent home, there was
another, older woman just down the hall
who had echolalia. She would repeat endlessly
whatever was the last thing she heard. She
had no control over this and I was never
sure whether she was even aware of it, or
how aware she was of anything at that point.
She just sat in her wheelchair, her head twitching
gently from time to time, repeating her words
like she was trying to memorize them.
Orderlies and candy-stripers would stop
in her room periodically, when they tired
of hearing the same thing repeated in that flat,
uninflected voice, and give her new words.
One day I passed her room and heard her
saying: asshole, asshole, asshole, asshole.
Someone's bad idea of a joke I thought.
Curious orderlies and candy-stripers arrived
but none of them did anything, just stared
as though they'd never seen her do this before.
Then I saw a nurse hurry down the hall
and enter the room. Who did this? she called
out loud. this, said the woman, this, this, this.
Instinctively the nurse turned toward her
and hissed, Shut up already! The woman

then switched to already, already, already.
The assembled staff stifled their laughter.
The nurse froze, realizing what she'd done
then smiled, and quietly said to the woman,
"Good afternoon" and the woman proceeded
to flatly greet us all for the rest of my visit.

Like Patchen

(for Mike James)

He chose an abstract painting
for the cover of his new book
because it reminded him of Patchen.
And it works well, that cover.
But Patchen was always figurative,
even if the figures were distorted
and grotesque, the surreal occupants
of fairytales and nightmares.
Still, Patchen's creatures were never
threatening or dangerous, they
were almost cuddly like plush
stuffed koalas, newborn weasels, and
broods of kittens with claws they
haven't yet learned to use judiciously.

And then there are the poems.

Spring By The Calendar

Overcast yesterday promised rain
But reneged, setting the stage
Then failing to deliver the drama.

Clouds passed on toward other,
Distant geographies where they
May deliver our rain as snow.

Irises already emerged from a
Raised bed of overgrown succulents
Continue with their own agenda.

Freshly pruned roses catch sun
Where tangles used to choke.
Buds greet the morning light.

Looking like yesterday but stripped
To bare sky, what must spring deliver
Just because the calendar turns a page?

Out of Place

If you feel out of place,
let me tell you about the tomato
plant I found growing
on a gravel bar by the river.

A seed from someone's picnic fell,
germinated, and took root
in the sparse dirt the flood
had swept between the pebbles.

The plant is thriving, bears
four ripe tomatoes. I left
them for the critters and for other
wanderers to marvel.

Missed Call

I cycle along Salem Avenue.
The trees are resplendent
with October leaves.
The way home is all downhill.

My phone rings. Vivaldi,
her ringtone. She left
four weeks ago. I still cannot
bear to enter her room.

My hand reaches for the bag
in the basket, fumbles
with the zipper –
I fly

over the handlebar, crash
on the asphalt. Something sharp
scrapes my thigh. Something hard
slams into my ribs. Stunned,

I crawl to the curb. Breathe.
Check for broken bones.
A car slows. Are you okay? I nod.
Later, I pedal the rest of the way home.
I did not get to pick up her call.

Every Time You Leave You Take a Sliver of My Heart

You back out of the driveway
in your little red car.
I stand by the garage and wave,
then I step quickly inside
so you won't be distracted
when you turn onto the street.

I walk upstairs,
pull the sheets off your bed,
collect your towels. I find
a lone white sock on the floor
and one of your vegan yogurts
left in the fridge.

I eat some cold pasta,
watch the clock,
wait for the phone to ring.

JOHN MACKER

snake time

I can't imagine a snake wondering about the word yes.
-Charles Bowden

summers years ago after it rained,
we'd bask in the twilight of snake time
one would shimmy out into the open
warily probing the air with her flicking
sentient tongue, decrying nothing
her diamond back as illustrative
as a mural
she wore the skin of the desert
she social distanced she
shed the sun like a coat of many colors

we coexisted we shared the news
of planet time in collaborative
still life peace
most nights she disappeared
& we'd listen to Mingus pluck out one
immortal soul of a note after another

in the news today the latest gun battle is words
we walk in flames to the voting booth
we meditate in our national emergency
I can tell it's that time because all the moisture
has been leeched out of the air

we awaken & then take cover
she crossed our path one morning like
a river that's sold its soul to the devil for a
moment of silence
not so much as a rapacious
whisper between us not on this planet
not this parched summer
no sentient being a stranger

Wild Blessings

Sitting here is a temporal abstraction,
as American as a guitar named "Trigger."
Two turkey vultures, mercifully illiterate
seraphim of smoke, soar over the nearby

petroglyph cliffs with their swastikas and
obscenities, a fixated rufous hummer
darts in and out of its own shadow.
Under the lilac my oldest dog absentmindedly

digs her own graves. Watching her, I realize true
enchantment is assuming today leads to the next
and the next and my ticket to however long it
takes is paid in full. Over the years my anonymity

has grown promiscuous, so, feel free to invent
a story like "Sam Beckett, Lover of Coyotes" or
sit here naked with me in this river's
calm pocket, an interlude and all of its sequels.
The pyrocumulonimbus cloud erupting over the
mountains is this spring gone mad torching
its own fate. The sun is a pomegranate. The sky ashen
like abused flesh, the smoke, in all of our openings

and closings has deposited an icing of rust on our
bones. These days are having their howlings,
their blaze in court. My dog moves from one shadow

to another, every new day names itself exodus or inferno.
Muir wrote if we hang out with the wild blessings
long enough that time will not be subtracted from
the sum of our lives☐ a wild blessing like the
acetylene sweetness of my wife's lips will see me

through the brash unknown. With our backs to the fires
no matter what we'll improvise, we'll orientate,
we'll obey nature as she struggles with her coarse
song, her sweet ruins, her shelters in place.

Moab

The military calls MOAB
the mother of all bombs
"massive ordnance air blast" bomb is
also step-mother of all bombs
moab is the motherfucker of all bombs
moab wasn't cut out for motherhood
but was forced to become a mother anyway
moab is the mother of all orphans
moab is swollen with loathing
and fear and nurses terrorists
a monstrous hybrid of the feral and
the civilized, moab is the mother lode of all ordnance
if moab visits Machado's grave, with a
frenzy she/he'll wipe out the future of his death

moab is non-nuclear, non-nutritional, non-
nurturing neo-blasphemous, androgynous
nether regions' goddess of ghosts blasted out of its
mind on end times' nursery rhymes
I am, she is, he will, we are beyond all recognition.
"Don't not ask for mercy," Bly said.

gangster's moll blowing hot and cold sweet apocalypse nothings

Moses died in the land of moab near the Dead Sea.
Moab, the incestuous son of Lot,
Moab, you are not our mother
Earth.

lost division

we would pedal our bikes
trudging the gravel that was mostly dust
of marquette ave
squat boxes and single wides

that one weird kid's parents
kept a donkey in the pen out back
and chickens that would
scatter at a call of "shitters!"

that stray dog always following
waiting for someone to drop something
waiting for someone to drop

there was the weird dude
in the tarpaper shack on the edge of the woods
who never came out
but to put empties on the porch
and shoo any of us away
who were brave enough to snoop

we were looking for anything
under those endless sycamores
we knew something had been lost
years ago
decades ago

and the trees
the road
the houses
the families
were still trying to figure out
what was missing

and we were just young enough
to be naïve and bold enough
to think we could save the world

if you followed the gravel and dirt long enough
you'd end up on pavement

THE SUBDIVISION

we always said it in reverent capitals
because that's the place where it hadn't been lost
not all of it at least
not yet
there the patchy grass was still kind of green
and there were a few
honest to god real basketball hoops in driveways
not the metal rings nailed to trees back our way
we marveled at how a kid might skateboard
were they so inclined

and we convinced the one boy to get his parents
to give us the scrap wood in their backyard
and we cobbled a bike ramp

in the field just south of

THE SUBDIVISION

we rode that ramp the whole summer
gravel kids and pavement kids together
and no one laughed when someone bled
and someone's mom always had kool aid
when it got too hot

and when we pedaled back to our
lot of dust and dirt
shutting drafty front doors
and closing our eyes
something had been found

m

when we met
he was living with his cousin
at the end of the hall

i tried to take his side
on everything
but he was always
so angry
then again
i suppose that'll happen
if your mom
shoots herself in the head
from the park bench
while you're tossing a frisbee

we got drunk a lot
talked music and movies
he dug goth metal and
horror flicks
i was more into grunge and
arthouse stuff
one night a case of red stripe in
he tried to sell me on the
artistic merit of
manson's golden age of grotesque and
freddy vs jason
i equally tried to convince him of that
peach gb album and
sideways

we did a lot of wobbly agreeing to disagree
after his cousin got tired of it all
he got a room in a duplex with some dude
way older and much more mature than us
then there was that big party
where i passed out on the floor
and someone pissed on the rug
and someone else
broke their arm out on the deck
and that was that

he moved somewhere else
only saw him once after that
he'd shaved his head
met a girl with a shaved head
seemed good

trickle down

little drummer boy roy's little sister
regularly ragged on the upperclassmen
especially those in
their cousin's hand me downs
windbreakers and jeans and starter jackets
that were last popular
when king george the first
was still mind wanking about the presidency

and i never understood where she got off
seeing as she wasn't cute
or funny
or really a nice person
and her older brother
nor their parents
seemed to give much of a shake about her

but then
maybe that last part
was all the answer needed

Vines

whispering syllables
remind me of cautious secrets
where words lack dimension
and darken
what lies behind the eyes
when actions are disguised
in symbolic interactions
tangled in a system of reasons
that don't rhyme
like vines clinging inside minds
with inconsistent timing
for the many who had
to endure a divergent walk
when gravity denied an exit

Wild Seeds

through harvested fields
surviving dusty solitude
between rows and rows of rich soil
farmed and plowed and considered

steps leading beyond
the open and closed field gates
on and on till gates are left behind
and paths open to large spaces
of flowing dreams
where wild seeds grow
and create the only place
with no need for opinions

Hijinks

liberated minutes
and unconfined lies
line hours of spoken conversation
in a back and forth hijinks
cascading into wild labels
opening discourse between
revealers of truth for not giving
into fables that confuse
and refuse to lower frustration
feeding into the gaps
and not refuting
the tags and tickets
to lost jazz and sweet tea
compositions inside
the balconies of minds
pushing notes to break free
and allow the mystic beats
and notes
to rise beyond occasions
and beyond time

KERRY TRAUTMAN

Birds of Belle, Missouri

Swallows swoop wild grass
oxeye daisy fields
like crop dusters sensing just when
to yank flight levers up.

Dozens of hummingbirds tongue
plastic feeder juice then chopper off
toward the Gasconade River.

Pileated woodpecker big as a raven
percusses barnwood.
Swallows allow it alongside
their persistent in and out and in.

Turkey vulture ruffles air like flicking
bedsheet up and over mattress,
then lands, grip wobbling branch
20 feet from my head.

Two dark hawks cry sharp
from dead treetop, taking turns
soaring over gurgling creek bed
like brown kites.

Whoever you are,
you called just twice,
and from somewhere near.
I have no answer.

Mortar

Avoiding I-70 construction, instead on US 40—
little sister parallel just south—driving through
single-stoplight Lewisville, Indiana—
population 366, total area a quarter mile.
We pass their 1902 opera house—
haunted, brick, with iron-framed storefronts,
on the grounds of a burnt-out 1893 building.

In Ohio, two garage bands share a bassist,
play their first-ever gigs before the poets read
in the backyard of a 1915, brick, former mansion
in Toledo's Old West End. Earnest, jumping as they
strum and whip long hair off faces, drummers
dutifully banging beats to lead the way.

The tiny opera house's sign advertises
its next show is RENT, and I imagine all the
Mimis, Marks, and Rogers in fishnets or scarves,
prepping audition songs in farmhouse attics,
belting Glory to the unseen rafter bats,
tractors and mac trucks rumbling walls
in place of the D train.

The backyard band kids hawk t-shirts
for gas money, pack-up cords and amps,
flirting with girls who ask to pluck their strings
while the poets take their turns at the mic.
Cigarette butts flick to the cracked concrete patio
and hostas, as a finch alights on a brick parapet.

We listen to each other pretend ourselves
over traffic whoosh, sirens, and feedback squeals.
Mortar crumbles to the ground, but bricks
don't fall just now. Asphalt splits from July heat and
weight of chassis, but roads hold another week. And
something about a bunch of 17- and 20-year-olds still
wanting to be rock stars means everything will be ok.

All Roads Lead to The Gasconade River

Life gifts us with versions of ourselves.
Will you be the braid-tail horse
who leaps the fence then shits
on the road leading to freedom?

Most major roads lead to water eventually.
You'll spot the treeline in the distance.
Close enough, you'll hear it.
Follow the gurgle and heron.

Some creeks flow every day
right across narrow roads which
somehow don't erode. Trust
your wheels to splash you right through.

Will you be the hummingbird lapping
sugarwater through a plastic bloom,
or will you risk buzzing away toward liatris
and larkspur on the opposite bank?

When a dead tree limb snaps
crack and gives way, falling to the river
it doesn't ask which way is downstream
which way up. It figures it out.

Some hills need 4-wheel drive.
Some only need the just-right touch on
the gas, the wheel, the ideal weight of
the folks beside you in the car.

Ask a friend which way to the river,
and let them lead you there, down a steep
gravel road, through a thicket, past a horse
who asks for a quick pat. Give it.

Some Long Ago Summer

Once upon a time I slept with a woman
who worked a few months at the group
home I run, but only after I fired her
for a no call no show weekend that left
the shifts severely understaffed. Next day,
we ran into each other on the subway,
rode through Manhattan together,
hugged goodbye. Four days later,
Denise waited for me outside work, went
all the way home with me. After fucking
the night away, we went to the diner
for breakfast. Grits for her, home fries
for me. We ended up at the schoolyard.
She took me down low, bumped me
with her lovely ass, while I tried
to ignore my hard on. I kept the score
close, but always won. She was younger,
I was older. I had money, she had none.
I was lighter, she was darker. She was
beautiful, I was not. We never could agree
on a radio station. We both liked Al Green,
but never the same songs. She loved
the back to back black shows on NBC
Thursday nights, I preferred Law
and Order. She never read my poetry.
I felt her rap rhymes silly and forced.

She liked things rough and hard, I liked
to watch my cum slide slowly down
her dark inner thighs. I didn't know
if she was hoping to get her job back,
looking for some kind of love or a few
weekends of outside the neighborhood
fun. I wasn't doing any thinking at all.
Just last week, she was standing in line
at the corner bodega. Coffee for her,
Snapple for me. She still looked good.
Me, worse than before. Once, she said,
she saw me walking by in some long ago
summer as she sat in a shady park rocking
her baby for an afternoon nap. She said
I never looked her way, but she knows
if I did I would have stopped, leaned
down for a soft quick kiss and told her
that her daughter was as beautiful
as she is. I smiled, knew she was right.

John And The Teenage Couple

While everyone at the group home
races through dinner in fifteen
minutes or less unable to forget
their years spent in Willowbrook,
the other patients who snatched
the food off their plates, John
takes hold of the serving dish
and fills his plate carefully, neatly
separating meat from vegetables,
mashed potatoes pushed far away
as possible. He whispers to ten
with each bite, lets the food
tumble past his Adam's Apple,
stabs another forkful, pauses
on the way to his mouth, surveys
the room for signs of danger before
bringing the food past his lips.

At neighborhood stores, he stands
in front of the floor-to-ceiling,
refrigerated glass case or stocked
shelves, rubbing his hands, mulling
over this life and death decision
until he reaches down, grabs a pack
of Yankee Doodles. He walks
to the counter glowing. Hello,
my name's John, what's your name.

The guy behind the cash register,
head burrowed into his cell phone
grunts, dollar fifty. John digs
his wallet out of his pocket,
holds it close to his chest, picks
a wrinkly bill from its sleeve. One
by one, he places pennies and dimes
on the counter, counting the amount
out loud as a teenage, hand-in-hand
couple saunters through the door.

The girl in tight ripped jeans, nipples
pressing against her cut off tee, lingers
up front, running her fingernails
across breath mints and gum, trying
to make eye contact with the guy
behind the counter as her boyfriend
roams the aisles stuffing his pockets,
sliding a pack of cold cuts under
his shirt, inside his waistband.
I watch John slow down even more
while the folks waiting in line turn
to me. But I know John wants to do this
on his own. He doesn't like anyone
touching his money and he's hoping
the cashier will discover he's mentally
challenged, find a bit of pity and decide
he deserves free Friday night cup cakes.

Holidays

When the guy next door,
yells out, you think I'm happy
the baby cries louder.
I am surprised not to hear
either of the dogs barking,
the wife cursing back.
I turn my music louder,
Laura Nyro's Christmas
Beads of Sweat for this New
Year's Day. I flew home
from visiting Jesse yesterday.
Nearly twenty years since
I spent New Year's Eve
with him, his mom. Happy.
I remember he was sleeping
and we were in bed. Straddling
my hips and laughing, small
town City Hall fireworks flashed
through the window, across
her eyes. The guy throws
a couple of fucks against
the wall and the woman
hits him with a son of a bitch.
These days we hardly talk.
Emails to arrange, confirm
monthly visits. We rarely
raised our voices, but the strain,

the silence, strangled the breath
out of the room. Something
bangs against the wall, shatters
across the floor. The husband
screams again. The Northeast
is frigid and that makes everything,
me, feel lonelier. Sometimes, I miss
Jesse's mom, even though I know
day to day we never fit that well.
A door slams and I hear footsteps,
paws, scuttling down the hall.
I love Jesse and miss him
as soon as I leave, but realize
how much easier my life has been
not taking care of a special needs kid
moment to moment. I walk
to the window, watch snow fall.
The woman next door's face
is hidden behind the hood
of her fur lined parka. She's trying
to pull the leash tighter, smoke
her cigarette, unfold a tiny plastic
bag and bend to pick up two
piles of crap before it stains
the new fallen snow. I go
into my bedroom and before
I close my eyes, I hear a lock
unlatch, the guy next door's
even tone, Feel better now?

LINDA ROCHELEAU

Photojournalist

A man hands over his daughter
to a stranger. Returns to his city
to pick up arms. A woman
gives birth in a shelter.
Names her child Faith.
Suddenly, yellow and blue
mimic hope and courage.
The bombed dwellings peel
back like fresh wounds.
Reveal the familiarity
of sofas draped with
throws or bodies strewn
like rag dolls. A wife,
A child. A leg in designer
jeans and stilettos pokes
out of the rubble
A woman embroidered
in fear stares blankly
at the cam

The Wolf is at the Door

A coyote in a chino suit,
carrying attaché with
papers to sign, blood to let
and tears to dampen gleam
from his white incisors.
The cell phone rings
morning to night, automated
dispatches, digital torture.
What's next? A homeless
shelter, bowls of soup
served by the Junior League?
I will take to the road.
So little time to worry at
75 mph across the Painted
Desert on Route 66 - taking
the tarmac back to better times.
For awhile blue vistas, cheap
tacos, fields of poppy
amid quiet echo of canyon.
Then mountains form a cradle
or halo to circle desolation
and despair. Mountain Woman
I once was tagged by a mentor
walking the streets of Miami.
I sadly pictured missing teeth,
dirty feet, and clicked my heels
against the pavement.

Coming off the parkway, I find
a Cuban restaurant in the center
of town, familiar and assuring.
café con leche, arroz con pollo
and a churro, I'm ready for
rekindling and fire.

Dew Drop Inn

As dive bars go, this one rates
on title alone. Second only to
Asheville Yacht Club. Snuggled
in a mountain town, clientele
harbor sleeping bags and dogs
on leashes. I confess I've never
been, only because former
deranged neighbor, a regular
smashed in my door. 4 A.M.
fight that spilled into my living
room. I've been a barfly in my day,
South Florida. Alabama Jack's
welcome sight after winding
through the mangroves on Card
Sound Road. Once a clogger,
nothing like feeling the dance floor
shift and sway beneath your feet
on floating pontoons. Then off
to the Caribbean Club, Key Largo.
Catching the sunset on Florida Bay
with a Cuba Libre in hand anticipating
what night may bring? Hussong's
in Ensenada. The night my Dad
and husband curled into each other
in the back seat while I navigated,
a sweet Georgia girl, his wife, through
Streets of Tijuana and across the border.

They didn't question the gringos passed
out in the back seat but made us throw
bottles of Tequila into a pit and shell
out the last of our pesos.
Back to the Dew Drop Inn
where a visiting poet friend and I
end our Savannah pub crawl,
from Pinkie Master's
to Spanky's on River Street,
Live to tell All.

MACK THORN

Brando

It's just the way
She sings sweet Billy
In my ear
In this motel room
at the corner
of rock bottom and heartache
makes me feel like Brando
in a bathrobe.

Patio Season

Pizza and coffee
is an underappreciated
soft spoken
machete
that slashes at the underbrush
of my hangover blues

look to the sun
in search of guidance
tell me
old one
is it patio season yet?

Under toe

Skipping belches
across green glass
cider poured over braised dermis
cook me slow sweet river
make me tender

jumping fish
snatch dragon flies
midflight over Dresden
the closest they will ever get to heaven

dive from starboard
to nab that new hat
floating towards
a destination unknown

pour mass
into rubber boots
last time I seen him
he was with you.

ink12x20 feb4-22 by Normon J. Olson

KRISTOFER COLLINS

Trace

for Anna

Oh babe, you'd hate the view
from here. Oily puddles gurgling
in the sun and the rich butter-colored
paint peeling like rind from the curb.
No sign of a single green thing anywhere.
There are people, too; strangers wilted
and unprepared for the flash of hot rain.
Some young father dashes across Main hurrying
his baby home while everyone in this room
is smiling at each other like they mean it.
In time we all come to know how rare that is.
Truly. It's only ugly out there if I choose
to see it that way. Some days the breathing comes
easier, mostly the air is rotten. But it helps
just knowing you're there. And even though
it seems impossible you'll ever take a dirty dish
and rinse it off in the sink or hang a shirt
in the closet rather than letting your clothes
fall like weather all around our rooms
I do want you with me in all our accumulated mess.
Anna, the truth is I can't tell disaster
from success without first checking the look
on your face, watching the blood rise or fall,
my whole being tuned in to that radio in your chest
pumping out the only music I will ever care to hear.

Blues for Allah

I bought a Grateful Dead record
in Austin, TX some years ago,
Blues for Allah,
then succumbed to the sun.
I walked a long August stretch.
I wondered where the hell everyone was.
I was an idiot.
In Texas she drank something cool
in a wooden shack, tasting wonderfully
of pickles.
Is it true you were never that happy again?
I wrote a poem for my buddy Don there.
I heard music falling out of every doorway
but never went in.
Some days I can't help but wonder
why I didn't.
It's the same as anything I guess.
Just didn't care enough.
Sometimes I'm still awake too late into the night.
I look at my wife there and I am amazed.
What are you doing here?
How did this happen?
My kids too asleep soundly.
The intensity of all this breathing
almost lifting the house
into the empty sky.
Almost.

2022

We are not yet
done dying
no matter
what the news tells us.
Like the night
patiently waiting
for the sun to falter
this too hides
eager to strike.
You can hear it
practically purring
so happy it is
to remove us.
Stealing our names,
what we could have been,
done
given the knowledge
this was the last
meager chance
we had
to finally
get this shit
right.

DAWNE LEIKER

Photographs

I searched the photographer's work,
Looking for traces of him.
To see his image reflected in the lens
He knew his world through.

The black and white portraits of his town
Flattened, contained, clean photos of the dirty 30s.
The day Tom Mix and his horse Tony came to town.
Trucks at a standstill on Highway 40, side-lined by an afternoon
    dust storm.
Knobby-kneed boxers sucking in their guts, puffing out their
    hairless chests.

Then I glimpsed his shadow, lower right corner,
near the spare tire of a delivery truck.
He wore a fedora and pointed a camera
at two men in business suits, unloading appliances
for a mortuary/furniture store on Tenth Street.

Eighty years later, I walk his same streets.
A colorized, noisy version of his photographs.

It seems madness to think that
all but the youngest of his photo subjects is dead by now.
Gone the way of my own grandparents.
I miss how the young picnic-goers grinned,
carefree in the summer sun.
How the kids in caps and overalls, paraded down Main Street
in search of Easter eggs.

How the art students, cross-legged on manicured grass,
touched pencils to sketchpads, intent on objects I cannot see.

If I could, I would slide through the lens,
hair in soft waves, wearing a starched cotton dress.
I would stand with broad-faced, neck-tied men.
Flash a smile at the photographer.
Draw him out of the shadows, in clear view.

We wouldn't see another war coming.
We couldn't know an Easter egg hunter
would lie dead on a beach in Normandy.

If I could be in his picture, I could stand
in perfect stillness, until I see it all in black and white.

Evening News

Maybe, just maybe, the only good thing
about the good old days
is that they are done.
Great Depression. Done.
Great War. Done.
Done.

The day he died.
That was a good old day.
Too chilly, though, some complained.
Snow lightly dusting straw-colored grass.
Dr. Zhivago's icy phantasm
projected across the
Fox Theatre's screen.
Drive-in moviegoers
warming their fingers by the
snack bar electric heaters
between disappointingly sexless scenes
of "How to Seduce a Woman."

The day he died, the headline read:
"Boy, 3, Apparently Abandoned
to a Slow Death" –
A story
from 35 miles away
the Sunday night before.
A story
that made young mothers check the locks
and windows, darken their children's doorways,

watching for the gentle lifting
of a small chest tucked tightly under the covers.
A story
of two women raped and murdered
and a child left to freeze when
the murderer was done.

The civic-minded man ate
a poached egg on toast
that Thursday morning,
while across town a typesetter arranged
The story
and set the headline
in 36 point Times New Roman.

The civic-minded man met
a murderer that day.
Not the killer of the two women.
Not the killer of the boy, 3,
But the killer of
a 19-year-old gas station attendant.
The killer of others yet unidentified.
And the civic-minded man grew cold on the concrete floor
before paper boys tossed
tightly rolled newspapers
onto porch landings
as evening edged the light from the day

Those were good old days for men
who opened themselves to the possibility
of ripping lives apart. Good days for men
who drifted down shadowed

gray highways. Shaving bag of amphetamines,
Beretta pistol. From No known address.

But, today's a good day, too.
A good day
to not talk to strangers.
A good day
to stay in after dark.
A good day
to worry the children away from the
pack of dirt. Position them
small and compact in rectangular houses
Small and compact on milk cartons
'Til the good old days
 are done.

The thing about a shadow

is how it dupes you.
How it presses you against a wall beneath a full moon
begging you to make shadow puppets or
simply lift your middle finger
      because you are so fucked.
At noontime, you follow it south and it doesn't care that you
      creep along footless.
So, you head north and you're aware it's following you.
Turning to look for certain, though, would only make you
      appear witless.

One night, the moon through cloud feathers winked,
spotlit my begonias drenched in pink.
On the front step with a cheap red blend
I waited, breathless, for nothing to happen,
my hair wild lashing upon the breeze.
I flipped off the moon, hugged my knees,
raised a glass to the shadow on the wall.
Its outline primitive, dank, hollow,
painted there in muddy ink.
Suggesting I pour another drink.

Juggernaut

after Kahlil Gibran

your nation will not be your nation
but a raging river of white
        water floods   what you built
is now the enemy of the people

your fear will not be your fear
but the terror of the hierarchy
        two-tongued bearer of arms
false prophets of flags and songs

your freedom will not be free
you will worship your own freedom
        and wear it as a handcuff
how can a tyrant rule the free and proud

your first amendment will not be first
your mouth and fingers so broken
        from conjecture battles
of monuments and kneeling

your soul will not be your soul
until your chains are broken
        and thus your freedom when it loses its fetters
becomes itself the fetter of a greater freedom

Identity Disturbance

It was not a time of war
but she remembers the stone throwing

the carbon matter and needles
her clutching at nothingness

she could trace it back to his eyelids
trace it on his eyelids

the febrile nights and fraudulent days
their unison reading of the holy writ

it infiltrated her magical thinking
under a diminished milky way

but he owned the weapon of a savior
of terrorism and ghosting

she remembers the broken doors
and ice on her skin

the marauding into the darkness
they never even slept

For What It's Worth

The bombing started again——no big surprise,
more separation of mothers and children——

we're not the only country that can pull that off.
Some say it will be world war III but

it doesn't matter what you think about peace,
you're not John Lennon.

As a child I wore a POW bracelet for months
but I never knew whether the soldier came home,

then I lost the bracelet and my innocence.
I remember the day it was over we rejoiced

but we didn't know why,
we just started waiting for the next war

hoping we didn't birth
our sons in the wrong year.

A friend's child was born in an unlucky year,
when he died at 20 I whispered,

what a waste——
not
what a hero.

Eventually you wonder what it's like
to leave this war-loving planet.

Maybe it's a day worth looking forward to,
you wonder if the dead got out just in time.

SCOTT SILSBE

Philip Levine's Record Collection and My Grandfather's Old Dictionary

I know it's goofy, but here I am wishing
Phil Levine were still among us the living
and I'm wishing I had his phone number
so I could call him to talk jazz with him.
Even though he's been gone a good 7 years
and when he was around, I didn't have any
phone number for him—and even if I did,
he probably wouldn't want a random call
from me asking which Lester Young LP
he likes best, or which one by Billie Holiday.
I do wonder about his record collection though.
Part of me would be hoping that he'd say
that all jazz was meant to be heard live—
that recordings don't do the songs justice.
Though I didn't ever have his phone number,
I *did* find his address once. And I wrote him
to thank him for helping out my old teacher
who was struggling to find work and funding.
His return postcard sits on my Levine shelf.

But now I'm thinking about my grandfather,
my dad's dad, my Papa—thinking about how
I wish that *he* were still around, so I could
call him up. Maybe I'd talk to him about jazz
as well—see if he remembers seeing a band
playing dixieland at Tony Packo's in Toledo.
He loved dixieland. My Papa. 9 years gone.

I have some of his records kicking around.
Some with his name sticker still stuck on.
I also have his framed "Hillbilly Degree."
Just the other day, I got out the dictionary
I gave him one year at Thanksgiving time,
an *American Heritage College Dictionary*.
I had inscribed it to him on the first page.
After he died when we family members were
sorting through his apartment, I went through
his books. There was the *American Heritage*.
I flipped to my old inscription to him and there,
under it—"Thanks, Scott," written in his hand.

As Long As You Say My Name

The music stops and then there is the silence—
I believe I might be on the other side of things.
It's a mellow Sunday, warm for early March
in Western Pennsylvania and I have done next
to nothing with my day—save some breakfast
and reading of Whitman, Kerouac, Jack Gilbert.
The stereo going with Charlie Christian, Coltrane.
Birds chattering a little out my open windows—
the wind kicking up a bit and knocking around
some neighbor's wind chimes down the street.

Just now the sun was dropping some of its light
down onto my bed and it got me to remembering
you here in bed next to me—you taking a snooze,
maybe in the late morning or the early afternoon.
You dozing, me watching you, the sun playing off
your hair and parts of your face there on the pillow.
You waking and smiling to see me there with you.
Those brown eyes of yours looking back into mine.

I Had to Go to Dark Places

after Jason Molina

It's true, I have no idea what you are going through.
I have almost no clue what it's like inside your head.
Honestly, I'm not sure I want to know. I have enough
going on up in mine. But then this thing that happens.

I tell you I am having a rough go. And you say, "Yes.
I know." And right there in the parking lot with all of
that snow falling down around us, you start to crying.

And the complexion of this world changes a little bit.
So you are having a rough go, too. I don't know what
I can say or do for you. For us. For this place of ours.
Except to tell you, "I know," like you just said to me.

I had to go to dark places to understand my friends—
understand myself. We're all of us broken but healing.
And we're proof that the heart is a risky fuel to burn.

DANIEL W. WRIGHT

A Shitty Christmas

Bing Crosby played throughout Red Lion, a local fast-food chain that specialized in roast beef. James Francis sang along in the best Bing Crosby impersonation he could muster as he put food away in cold storage. His boss Michelle counted down the money so they could close early and spend Christmas Eve with their families. His impersonation wasn't very good, but it did put him in the holiday spirit.

James looked at the clock. It was fifteen minutes until close when James noticed a minivan pull up outside, and a family of four got out. James rolled his eyes in disbelief but changed the look on his face to happily greet the customers when they came in. The father of the family walked ahead of everyone else. His hair was greying at the temples, and he was dressed in a tan business trench coat, a buttoned-up shirt, and slacks that looked like they were being worn for in-laws. His wife seemed to resemble a church mouse. His children looked like they had been disciplined to never disappoint their parents.

The father walked up to the counter with all the swagger of a mid-twentieth century man to place his order.

"Happy holidays! How ya doin' there!" said the father.

"Doing great, sir," said James. "How can I help you?"

"Well, we were on our way to having Christmas with our family, and I realized that my kids have never had a Red Lion Tasty Cone! So, I was wondering if I could get four of those to go, please!"

"I'm very sorry, sir, but we put the ice cream up for the night. We're going to close in fifteen minutes."

"What do you mean?" the father asked.

"Well, we're about ready to close up the store to go spend the holidays with our families. I'm sorry, sir, but all we have left are a few pre-made sandwiches."

The father checked his watch before saying, "But it's only 4:45!"

"That's right, sir," James said. "We're closing at 5:00 to spend time with our families."

"Honey, let's just come back another time," said the mother.

"No, no, no, no!" said the father, raising his finger towards his wife and his voice towards James. "This is bullshit! You guys are still open, so you should have everything to offer any customer who wants it!"

The father's raising voice caught Michelle's attention, who stopped counting down the day's earnings in the back room to see what the commotion was.

"Hello, sir," said Michelle, "I'm the manager. Can I help you?"

"Yeah!" said the father, putting his hands on his hips. "I just came in here just to get four ice creams for my family. And your guy Friday here is saying I can't have them!"

"I'm very sorry, sir, but we put the ice cream away for the night," said Michelle.

"This is bullshit!" said the father. "I want my fucking ice creams, and I want them right fucking now, or I swear to God there's going to be hell to pay!"

"Hon, let's just…"

"No!" said the husband, sticking his index finger in

his wife's face a second time. "This is a matter of principle! I'm gonna get my fucking ice cream!"

Michelle knew there was no dealing with someone like him. She sighed and told James to get the cream out and turn on the Tasty Cone machine. James went into the freezer, closed the door enough to be out of sight, and punched the air. He knew it would take at least twenty minutes to get the cream to a state where it could be served like ice cream. James stopped kicking the back wall when he heard the door open and turned to see Michelle.

"I really hate to do this to you, but can you get the roast beef out and the curly fries. The guy now wants three fresh roast beef sandwiches and a large order of curly fries."

"What, the family's eating now?!" said James.

"No, just him," said Michelle.

"What?"

"He's demanding a meal because I tried to tell him that it was would take about twenty minute for the ice cream and he suddenly decided he's hungry," said Michelle. "Let's just get the guy his food and get him the hell out of here."

"What about the pre-made sandwiches?"

"He says he wants his food fresh," said Michelle. "Look, I'll make the food. You just get the ice cream going."

Michelle left to turn on the deep fryers, leaving James in the freezer. James pulled out his phone to call his sister, Amy.

"Hey," Amy answered.

"I'm going to be a little late getting home."

"How late?"

"I don't know," said James. "I gotta deal with some asshole

customer who came in last minute, deal with closing up, and then I can head out."

"Well, try to get home as soon as you can."

"I will," said James. "Tell Mom and Dad that I'll be late, but I'll be home soon."

"Okay," Amy said.

Amy had just gotten home that day from college, which had somehow made this Christmas more significant. Even though the exact same people were spending the holiday together like last year and the year before that. James kicked the back wall as hard as he could before grabbing the cream.

James and Michelle got to work prepping sandwiches, fries and ice cream. James wondered who it was that first came up with the mantra of "the customer is always right" and wondered if it was at all possible to kick that man in the balls. While the ice cream was getting ready, the husband sat at a table while his family watched him eat. The rest of the family drew their eyes to the floor while he ate.

"Kids, you want any of these fries? They're really good!" the father asked in a chipper tone. The kids shook their heads.

"Fine, more for me."

When the ice cream was ready, James put the Tasty Cones in a plastic container designed to hold them.

"What the hell is this?" asked the father.

"I'm sorry, is something wrong sir?" said James.

"My family and I want to have our ice cream here!" said the father.

"Honey, let's let them…"

"Stop!" the father said towards his wife, again sticking a finger in her face.

James held back his desire to whack the father across the face with the tray he grabbed, taking the plastic container for the ice cream and placing it neatly on the tray. The family went back to the table with the four ice creams.

"Kids, you all want your ice cream?"

The kids nervously shook their heads no.

"Suit yourselves," said the dad, eating all four cones. "Y'all don't know what you're missing!"

When the father was done, he got up and asked James where the bathroom was. James pointed the way. A few minutes later, the father came out, rounded up his family, and left Red Lion. James locked the door and finished wiping everything down, including the Tasty Cone machine all over again. Just as he finished, he heard Michelle scream. He went to see what it was and found her holding the men's bathroom door open and saw a giant shit with fecal splatter on the men's room floor. James ran to see if the minivan was still there. It was gone. He walked back to Michelle, who still holding the door open while looking away and covering her nose under her shirt. They both looked at each other, knowing who was going to have to clean this up.

MIKE JURKOVIC

The Girl and Her Parachute

The girl and her parachute
were a cute enigma
from the moment
she got in my car
six miles awry
of her landing.

Thanks for the ride she said,
her parachute strangely mute.
So unlike my mother-in-law
going rogue in Vegas.

But this isn't about
any mother-in-law
past or present.
This is about the girl
and her parachute,
who could have landed on my car
if the westerlies were true.

You go for the buzz because
all the rest is bullshit she said.
And in the sky above Awosting
two clouds were eloping.

Downtown Comedy Legends

Rummy Blinks and Gravel Duck would never be
the downtown comedy legends they sought to be
cos they stayed plush dealing dust
and doing favors for Toady Morocco,
a South Side pimp
who ran his ten blocks
w/a gunner's gaze.

I wouldn't fuck your sister for those two
he said w/o haste
and a benzedrine bray.
But they get the job done
ya gotta give 'em that.

Rummy Blinks and Gravel Duck
were a very thin thesis
to carve a case around but,
like the burning city itself,
a thesis just the same:
of drift and wreckage.
Wreckage and grift.

Yearbook

Frost's granddaughter
convinced me of my brilliance
as she held me between her legs
like I was the last poet on earth.

We were young so sex closed the deal.
Rock that girl and you were the next big thing
in the land of lettres. Bite her neck
and she read your words w/worship.

Hell, I could do that.
It was junior year n I
had spunk aplenty.
My tongue 'tween
her cleavage,
her lips on
my belly,
our fingers
tracing sweat.

I had a way w/alliteration
that was totally American
she said. My hands on her
feverish ass, foraging for
her fulcrum. Breathing warm along
her panty line. Their color that
of open sky.

MARIA VASQUEZ BOYD

We believe in miracles

I am told by my Father Reynaldo Cortez, we come from generations
of Curanderas and Healers

We believe in miracles

I am told by my Mother, Rosa that Grandmother learned what she
learned from her Mother, and her Mother's Mother
our Ancestors

Once during a raging storm under indigo skies
My Mother witnessed Grandmother gathering dried palms that she
placed in a clay pot on a table filled with photographs, copal and
candlelight

She carried the clay pot outdoors
And lit the dried palms with a match

Grandmother offered the burning palms to the cardinal directions
North
South
East
West

Whispering to Eh-heh-cote, the God of Wind
The end of Birth is Death
The end of Death is Birth

Eclipse

June 30, 1954; the longest total eclipse of the century occurred

My Mother, Rosa, her sister Josephine and their sister-in-laws Julie, Mary, and Rita were pregnant during a total solar eclipse on June 30, 1954.

It was the Aztecs who thought that an eclipse occurred because a bite had been taken out of the moon.

My Grandmother warned each of the pregnant women to stay indoors before, during, and after the eclipse so that the babies in their bellies would not be born with a bite taken out of its mouth like the moon.

My Grandmother then fashioned a chain of safety pins wide enough to cover one side of their abdomen to the other. Her beliefs were imprinted on the swollen bellies of each Mother.

I was told that Aunt Julie who was married to my Uncle Ruben, was "one of those modern women" who didn't believe silly Mexican superstitions. But on the day the solar eclipse arrived, Aunt Julie was seated in the kitchen of my Grandmother's house with the other pregnant women.

Aunt Julie rose from her seat, lunged for the backdoor, and stepped out on to the lawn before the others could stop her. The Mothers gasped as she reached for the safety pin chain from her belly and unfastened one end.

My sister Maria Antonia, was the first to be born followed by my cousins Mark, Arthur, Jeannie, and finally Michael.

Each baby was loved

Each baby was born in good health

Years later I smile as I look closely at family photographs of my sister and cousins born that year. In each of the five photographs each baby is held in my Grandmother's arms. She smiled her beautiful indio smile upon them as a blessing. Each tiny face revealed features defined by each family, my sister with her almond shaped eyes, Mark with adobe colored skin, Arthur born with the high Indian cheek bones of his Mother, and Jeannie, the cousin who bears a resemblance to a China doll.

But it was Michael who appeared agitated and unhappy in his photograph.

It was Michael who quit school.

It was Michael who was kicked out of his family's home after he lunged at his Father and pressed a shiny knife blade to his neck.

It was Michael who wandered at night and stayed in the shadows of day

Father Sky

A curious messenger holds the lightness of spirit
A spirit whose purpose brings good fortune like moonstone

The discovery of truth is inseparable from life
His words are as good as his deeds

He maps the migration of people
With spirals and circles

North
East
South
West

Under the blue shimmer of moonlight
The cluster of stars dance like children

New Word

I can barely rarely define
today its blast of flash bang
smoke-filled torrent tumbling
upon me like tsunami information
overload TikTok tweeting
my brain a dartboard
for influencers
who Dow-crash me
Putin-terrorize me
gasoline-price soar me
climate-exhaust me
I'm crawling with supply
chains all coiled like snake dens
like intestines knotted in pain
What new word could invent to
subsume my global agony
individual despair
existential angst—
a gray cloud eternal 3 a.m. daily hourly
throbbing as pulse as breath obstructed?
What new word can create
the salve needed to placate
   No—to alleviate
      No—to resolve
         No—to uplift
us in this world
our only world
seeking even
a scent of rain?

Planting in Dry Land

I'll grow me dry beans since what the hell else
is gonna sprout in a hundred and two

and the desert is dreaming about rain long gone
pinto and navy, kidney and black,

so down I dig, deeper than most,
to ferret what moisture hides under rocks,

and jam them bean shells at least thumb deep
and use my canteen to drench them some

before covering them up with dry dust mulch,
wipe my sweat on my chambray sleeve,

put my gimme hat atop my head,
squint at the sun glaring through cloudless skies,

then trudge back to my barn to sip on a brew,
and wait.

Existential Cataract

I had my eyes checked today.
It seems I've seen life through
cataract lenses all gray

and distracted, my periphery
dim my distance contracted
in shadows with edges myopic.

My soul's a corneal hole distorted
from what's rosy and pure
as if on day one of creation

my DNA missed the memo
about light's expiation
from darkness. So I've stumbled

past colorless mores. I'm all styes
of stigma. What should be black
and white, you see, for those enlightened

has degenerated my cataract
topography. I've become a
fathomless depth of moral opacity.

Sandlot

The blue-green ball field; the sage sandlot, the vert vineyard of vernal baseball players dotted the baseball diamond-like chicken-pox spots on Piccolo's boney cheeks. Beryl weeds and apple aquamarine grass littered the dead patch of beige where he was standing. He was a reluctant right fielder, slightly overweight, and constantly stuttering with a vexatious lisp. Big-lipped with gapped teeth standing in a baseball uniform with the name Pirates haphazardly embossed on the back, staring at the pitcher, hoping no Frankenstein-stitched lead balls come his way. But even if one of those hemetic sutured summer stealers came his way, he was trained in how to catch and properly toss one of those fatalistic flame-fastened fastballs back into the inner diamond.

The scalding, searing hot, thermogenic saffron sun was away that day, leaving a heterogeneous mix of Purbeck stone and Cornforth white portrayals in the sky. He wasn't sweating, plus the team he plays for sucks, so the likelihood of a ball coming to him was as slim as the chances that he would have sex with the women on the softcore porn channel. That's pretty much what HBO and Showtime were to him. He would stick his dick in the crease of pillows. Right there, in between the copper-painted pillow and the henna-stained pillow sheet.

To be back home watching glimpses of side boob and maybe a nipple was all he wanted. But it was his father who took him to Matthew Dickey and gave him the option of baseball or football because he couldn't do boxing for some reason. Maybe the slots were full, or maybe the thought of these muscular thirteen-year-olds juxtaposed with this slightly overweight lisping child was a bit too much for the coach to handle.

By the way, I'm that kid in the dirty Pirates uniform. 'Pirates' was our team's name. It's a funny name because we never stole anything, not one base. Some of us couldn't catch an STD, always dropping the ball like a British spy playing billiards with a KGB agent for the design of the atom bomb and then losing like Hilary Clinton. The good thing about baseball was that I didn't have to do anything, especially playing in the outfield. It was like being my other brother's first father. I'm here for a bit, I contribute nothing to the other players, and I reaped all the benefits if they succeeded. But unlike their biological-bum-dad, I had to stay there with the team until the 8-hour game was over.

It was like a workday that I had to pay for. Well, my dad had to pay, and he was willing to do it. He was like,

"You got to do something. Can't have you in the basement torturing insects and small animals, pissing under the stairs, and starting fires that you think we don't know about."

He only knows about some of those things. I reflected on these things as I stood staring at the beryl weeds and apple aquamarine grass that littered the dead patch of beige.

Cahokia: City of the Cosmos

    I went to the Cahokia City of the Cosmos lecture with my friend Moesha. The lecture was informative (which is a nice way of saying "boring"). One of the more interesting parts of the lecture was all the speculation. The lecturer theorized, or speculated, that a super Nova, which could have been the third brightest object in the sky, around the year 1006 AD, or C.E. for the atheists. According to the lecturer, this super Nova led thousands to Cahokia. Now, it also could have been due to drought, disease, and/or urbanization, but the lecturer was a spiritual man, as I found out later.

    During the question and answer period, there were many boring yet practical questions until one young lady asked if there were orgone generators at Cahokia. Moesha and I began to giggle as we assumed the lecturer was struck dumbfounded. The lecturer didn't have a clue what she was talking about, but I will explain it to you.

    Orgone is a pseudoscientific idea. It is esoteric energy or hypothetical universal life force, originally proposed in the 1930s by Wilhelm Reich. Orgone was the anti-entropic principle of the universe, a creative substratum in all of nature. Orgone was a massless, omnipresent substance, like ether, but more closely associated with living energy than inert matter.

    After the question and answer period was over, I wanted to ask the lecturer if the Mounds at Cahokia were used as ancient alien spaceship launch sites, but Moesha asked me not to. Moesha was going to ask the lecturer how often he was asked questions like that, but because Moesha had to leave, I decided to ask him her question. When I did, he said that question about the orgone generator was the first question of that kind that he had gotten. He went on to tell me a story about a frog.

One day when he was doing some work over at Cahokia, he moved the covering over an excavation site, and he saw a frog, the next day, it was a toad, and that toad stuck with him for the rest of the month. This happened in sequence multiple times, according to the lecturer. He went on to explain that frogs and toads are spiritual creatures. He believed that there were other dimensions, a spirit world possibly. He told me that he left clues in his lecture. At the end of the lecture, on the last PowerPoint slide, there was an image of a snake. See what I meant when I said that the lecturer was a spiritual man?

I ran into Moesha sometime after I finished talking to the lecturer. I told my friend, and now I'm telling you.

The Job

I'll tell a story like a perforated colon coming into your scattered brains. A loose grouping of buckshot further splattering thoughts, shattering veins. Which are eviscerated like you woke up at 5:40 am. Threw on the dirty clothes you wore the day before because you work in a warehouse, and if anybody judges the way you smell, especially anybody over 30, then they seriously need to question the decisions they made in life. Peregrinating out of the house into the chilly natural standpoint. "Peregrination," yeah, you ain't never heard of that word. It's from the French word for pilgrimage because it is truly a religious experience to work where I worked.

Not the enlightening experience where you see Jesus healing a school of lepers with leukemia in Lithuania. It is the kind of religious experience where your mom makes you take a bath in the dirty bathwater that everybody just used. But you don't take a bath; you just stare at the greywater, waiting. Waiting until you were there long enough to tell a believable lie. Then your parents drag your stinking little body to church. Smelling like ass through those thin cotton nylon pants. Going to work at that warehouse was that kind of religious experience.

Got in a caliginous Camry coup. Started the car and turned on NPR because I'm an inept bleeding heart. Liberal enough to complain about poverty and able to hate on our capitalist overlords who would still be filthy rich even if they invested in the underprivileged a little more, but still enough of a piece of shit to not have an issue with unpleasant design. That's what cities do to force the homeless away from places where we can see them. Like park and bus stop benches with the armrest in the center that makes it hard for people to sleep there unless they have spines that curve like a parabola.

Needless to say, I'll say it anyway, I didn't want to work. I was mad, hot as Syrian civilians firebombed by Assad. Hot as a Philly helicopter bomb dropped on kids and they mommas in urban brick and stone buildings. But you know what? This was my last day of work, and when I got to work, I was going to tell my supervisor, Don't test me! Like I told the ACT Procter. By the way, I did very poorly on the ACT. I suck at test-taking. Not sure if my poor performance was from not studying or if it was from me randomly filling every circle, so I couldn't possibly be wrong. You ever make images with the ABCD answer dots? I drew a snake before I filled the rest of the circles in. Those graphite circles were a clue, a road to my future. I drove down that road north to Morgoth. Down streets caliginous, malicious as my style is stylish as a pile of platinum scripture. These streets were bestial, like that place where Frankenstein's monster fights against Herbert West's monsters with a hatchet. That's where we get the term 'bury the hatchet." The supervisor was that which lurked in the cinereal cubicle. An unctuous prison encampment where he launched nooses. He was one of those creatures from the Isthmus on vacation in Sheol. I seriously considered pooping on a portrait of his family, but he was so monstrously hideous that he would have thought that I cleaned it.

I arrived at work early, disheveled, appearing derelict, revealing the badge, the chain to this unctuous Isthmus prison encampment. I ambulated up the stairway, which was pale and never-ending like a depressed Shahrazad reciting Silvia Plath's poetry on the gallows. See! That 'nooses' metaphor makes sense now, right? In the office, one gets the BENS because one is suffocated under mountains of paper and fountains of files. I crept into the supervisor's cubicle. I really wanted to tell him that he was a terrible sexist gerbil man-monster face doo doo-headed, shit-nosed manatee-mouthed molasses screwdriver, gerrymandered fast spasm.

These would be the torpedoes I'd spit. Grammatically extraordinarily seditious syntax. But I just asked the ogre for an assignment, and as I was drowning on the production floor, he sent me to the darkest, coldest storage room in the building. The place where we kept the burn files. Files burned in a previous conflagration. Shelved in boxes on a steel meshed floor. He had a gaze as caliginous and malicious as my style is stylish as a pile of shit. Truly felt like a lukewarm pile of shit picked up like dreams dashed and crumbled into the final level of Sheol. I resided in the final circle, ice bathing with the devil.

PAUL KONIECKI

Geometry and Poetry and Proximo

Everything we knew of Rome
We learned watching
Oliver Reed from bed
Proximo exhorting

"The mob is Rome"
Love espousing a different kind
Of going to the mattresses
Geometry and Poetry

Mystifications allowing us
To oscillate between
Self-defense
And self-definition

One Greek
For measuring the Earth
The other Latin for weighing
Everything else

a cluster of hippos

is called a crash
hippopotamus
from the greek meaning
river-horse therefore
a group of hippos is also
a horse crash tamus being river
all hooves and manes and galaxies
glorious colliding energy
stored trapped and releasing
nina simone said an artist must reflect
their times and in these post post pandemic
days where
from my hardly-living room
no hippos can be found
i am a portrait of a twinkie
truer still a landscape of a
dilapidated twinkie factory
bursting with unsalvageable cream
signifying the damnation of bricks
and the moral shortsightedness
of preservative
to sail the seven seas
count to three
take a breath
it's all one ocean anyway
one singer one song
one pole one fish
one whale one wailer
one irreducible we

deck the tarot with rhapsody

I dreamed Everette Maddox is a character in the next Wes Anderson film
—Brett Ardoin

the only thing more than a voice

are the words that it
is saying

with them carbon dioxide for the trees
and praise be on the butterflies

look
the hummingbird
and the hibiscus
are making love

over by the dumpster
we
society's newly evicted

pasodoble

in lieu of working showers
pray for rain
listening to seu george
cover bowie's rebel rebel
and you snore steve zissou dreams
of carrying
the novel coronavirus
to the bottom of the marianas
trench in a bathysphere

and everyone
is safe and clean

it's decided then
make me a stolen cartouche
in a wes anderson film
lower my body onto a park bench turned sepulcher
melt in the fullest harvest moon

stand a single birthday sparkler
in a field of new mown grass
swaddled in a shroud of acquiescing fireflies
alive and quivering
for in that cloud
of light and winged insects
i dream of everette maddox
sleeping under newsprint

studying bobbins
and thimbles and a chance for the heroic
in the needlecraft of words

the monsters under your bed are real

and they are forever waking.
They move slowly, undetectably
crawling with spiky knees
or gooey tentacles. Hair grows
from their ears, eyes like polished
onyx drink from the black cosmos
extravagantly--missing nothing--expanding
and receding with every rise
and collapse of your breathing.
This one knows exactly how much
water is left in the cup by your bed.
The number of pleats in the sleeves
of the astronaut that wanders
across your walls from Pluto
to Saturn to Mars. That one counts
the dust particles that have been collecting
since your first communion. Craves a bite
from the succulent bacon and cheese
sandwich you left in the closet
during the last Spring downpour.
You have been listening
to their whispers so long
you no longer notice, like the buzz
of the refrigerator or the same
joke the cockroaches have been
telling for years. Chittering.
They are lonely monsters and want
to share their dirty songs from Church

Camp, their opinions on Simon Cowell
and Oprah, their recipes for bad clam
and mushroom soup casserole, furry
sour cream and Fig Newton stew.
It is not unwise to be afraid,
but that doesn't mean you can't
be congenial. Just keep your jammies
buttoned, one hand on your waistband
and the Gumby and Pokey nightlight
plugged in.

Plummeting

I fell asleep watching television and left
my chair for the last smoke before bed,
outside where it was damp and air sopping
from eruptions of rain that ended just as
abruptly. Droplets blistered leaves
and porch lights became vague vapor

halos. Veronica my neighbor sat beneath
the mailboxes smoking for a few moments
before she noticed me too. She was tipsy
in a pleasant way (as she and her roommate
often were) and though I wondered, it seemed

too soon to ask if they were lovers. Ruth came
down and for awhile we compared bracelets.
She was breathy and rapturous, running back
to find the calm ebony Buddha that anchored
the front mantel of their home. We rubbed

his ponderous belly when she returned,
where I'd been visiting with Paco
for twenty minutes. We'd never met before
and I might have assumed he was Veronica's
Dad. But you never introduce your father
as a friend. The poison of his most recent
divorce soured his gut, the one item salvaged

a statue of Icarus. "Even though he's falling,"
"you can see there was nothing else to do."
Paco had never known the cost of eggs

or bread or the pleasure of relaxing
with the newspaper. His grown children
wanted nothing to do with him and he knew

his wife was a bitch but to him, she was
a princess. "There's no shame in pursuing
a woman on your knees," he said. "If only
for the chance to partake in that radiance."
Of course I didn't tell him. In Mexico
they say the best listener is a stranger

because you can disclose the details
of every crime, every irrevocable choice
that continues to diminish and convict
you. "You're a good listener," he told
me. I didn't explain it was the hour
that came every evening that left me

wrecked and infected with regret.
Another sloppy remark or revelation
that jeopardized grace
of love returned. I didn't explain
how the ascent he fashioned for us
with plume and harness
would drown us together.

Black Diamonds

I'm not sure how you ignited this smoldering
clod of fossil fuel clenched beneath rib staves,
layers of tense, sinewy chest muscle.
Is it radiant, stewing magma, like a vibe
from my dad, those comical goggles
he wore for astigmatism, just like yours?
His hair a lunar eclipse in November,
or the sky when God is finally gone
and through. Maybe you remind me
of a boy I betrayed. Not nearly as splendid,
I confess. I couldn't believe how easy
it was to just close him off. Another iron bandage
to slow the beating down. It is not sufficient
to say that I am bad news. Though you couldn't
find better company when grain and time
and distillation have turned your blood to ash
and molasses. I'm worse than strychnine,
frosty stillbirth on a farm where they track
cloud and tide but ask no help from the Father
of breath, of light. I can only say I've known
this since the night I made myself ask
you, since the Christmas of my first phonograph
and Superman cape. I am filled with chuckles
and snot and solace and bad songs. I am filled
with steam and smoke and teeth and clay and bones.
I am filled with catastrophe and disaster; earthquake
and hurricane, black diamonds spilling
from my lips.

TONY BREWER

The Business End

I'm into war porn
know the models
by their payloads

When someone else does
evil when we do
it's acceptable

I sound so political
as if saps sign up
because they feel something
wrong

Can you imagine
the might of an empire
agreeing with you
& vice versa?

But then I'm trained
to interrogate a country
not stare slack jawed
into the abyss of its barrels

questions answered by calling
History moments
the pendulum swings

right or left

always passing
through the middle
like a wrecking ball

attracted by visuals
titillated even
by a passion for machinery
the beauty of weapons

How could I resist?

Home for the Holy Days

I try being smug
at the very real diner
thinking about my old haunts

Not this one
a new brewery sprung up
in my hometown

because every little town has
one it's partly why going
home is always weird

Back to not being listened to
Haven't done a thing since I was 12
My perfect silence

On my way "home" home
ambling into a non-Applebee's
experience for once

Treated like an old man
humored and placated
leaving a big tip:

Don't live so far away
you can't get home
when they need you
and realize sooner than later
they really don't need you

Loving the job

My furnace guys jerk
each other around
friends longer than marriage
and they spar "like
an old couple" says Ron
I was thinking comedy duo routine
the artificial back-and-forth
of bickering without malice
requiring no setup
You know how this one goes:
old couple fighting
telling you it's normal
means they've lost the words for love
if they ever had them
Grown into the grade school
shoulder punch
Insults raining like tiny kisses
but an occasional peck on the cheek
Mom and Dad were like
nothing I'd ever laughed at
She hysterical in his
invisible stranglehold
while he bitched out her every move
Me in the belly of it
burning gently like a pilot light
That's how I relate to people
Are you serious or joking?

Did I buy a ticket to a show
or are we related?
Jokes aside they do good work
with one-year labor guarantee

CAROLYN SRYGLEY MOORE

Running out of Gas

Picked up some apples the Lethe
   & drove on on
Highways of lions lapping blind milk
From hearts

I drove til
The gas tank
Was empty.

   I'm
Glad she's not living now
There are a few facts
   I'm glad death spared her
Shiny soul
The brim of a desolation
A discontent

That familiar winter.

   Indeed. I ran out of gas
Somewhere between convenience stores
Route 67. The nor'easter is coming.
My friend is feral
Or fetal
   & I too could scarcely rise
Today

For unlike the sun
        I have a semblance.
  I have choice
Ducking my face into drifts
Oncoming. If I knew how to bear arms
If I wasn't considered crazy
        I'd cross the seas or drop
Drop
Via a parachute darkly winged
On those streets
        Built
In the Ninth century.

History is everything.
Naming is everything. The deer
Flashes her tail
& I am the consequence of
        What but the coupling
A man & woman
Who lived & dissented &
Carried arms
Piloted planes
Played nocturnals
        Keyboard dream Chopin.

Graffiti

We lean back
Into debris fire gutted kitchen walls
 A house a
River a dock we
Glimpsed from
The beltway. A Roman numeral
    Clock between us.

1.   We smoke blow smoke rings
Watch graffiti shift morph

The tongue an instrument of curled
    Split hollows.

-        We lean
Eucalyptus & our headstrong natures
Eclipse the sweet
A genetic intensity. Sheer pink

        Spaceships are captured
In this river see
    the balloon resistance
Parachutes torn by rock
& they who don't know
What reality is. Individual.
    Not Roswell but a watery
Reflection

The fire gutted houses by rivers &
Graffiti
      We scribed by crayon
The evidence
    In pebble & spilled blue rune
Our mutual exile.

(This is where the poets play)

Wicks, Shifting // As He Speaks

It's hard to not take it personally
That far bend in the river

Bundles of bread & blankets left
There for the friends

The wick of a candle shifting
Like lace in the wind

Fear can be a place of consolation
Knees tucked to the chin

Nearly fetal
Feeling the human crease between

Your own ribs
The present rib the missing rib

The fire invents itself
Over & over again

Moonlight traces the bundles
Waiting in the river niche

We will never he says to the world
Never run out of love & respect

The most necessary freedoms
An uncensored moonlit blood

Moon hallow's Eve ghost
   Montage lingering

Tongue cut
On barbed wire

Brandy Ambles into Detention

I missed my bus to come here. I hope
my boyfriend will pick me up or I'll have
a long walk. This is the only place I can
do homework. You have no idea what life's
like at my house. We live in a motel room.
It's a big room, but I have six brothers and one
sister. My Mom and Dad are rarely there, so I
babysit. My brothers are demons. Better hope
you don't get them. The baby has fallen off the bed
three times, and the last time had to go to hospital,
and it's ALWAYS noisy. We go outside during
summer because the air conditioner doesn't work,
but in winter, Mom won't let us outside in the dark,
and that means I can't walk to a library to type my essay.
You'll have to take it handwritten 'cuz I can't get here
before school either. We're going to an apartment
when my Daddy gets some overtime. He had a good job
as a mechanic. We lived in a house with a fenced-in yard
but he got laid off. Now he's at Walmart until he can find
another mechanic job. At least it's quiet in here, but I
don't see how I can ever read a whole novel unless
I read it right here. My history teacher said if we don't
know history, we're doomed to repeat it. Yeah, I failed
history and have to take it again. I'll probably be here a lot.

Dead Space

I. Hypnagogia

Before sleep, we float
in a hammock of captured breath.

II. On Hold

If not the song you want
to fast forward, shell rush.

III. Empty

The mile walk on a gravel
road with a gas can.

IV. Snowstorm

Staring into a snowstorm
is falling through a long silent ride.

V. Elevators

A dozen squeeze in and punch
floors below yours.

VI. Binge

You will not remember that night
no matter how many prompts.

VII. Floating

Sailboat bobs and waits for wind
to carry it from unexplained quiet.

VIII. Spring dirt

Inhale, and the world
gets bigger.

IX. Between Walls

Twelve inches between, you will not hear
your neighbor sneeze or scream.

X. Underwater

The quiet barracuda hover
when they arrive to watch.

XI. Between Rings

Waiting on 911
after your spouse falls.

XII. Waiting Room

Before the doctor arrives
to say how surgery went
and after.

In Line at the DMV

We inched in line, snaked around stanchions,
and spilled into the parking lot, waiting.
We scrolled and yawned. We jabbered

into our phones and clutched documents
we needed for a new plate or license renewal
when she shrieked from the back, *What's*

the holdup? How long does it take to hand someone
a f'ing sticker? Someone's in danger here!
She yanked a baretta from her purse,

bellowed, *I wanna talk to your f'ing boss!!,*
and shot a few rounds into a mulch bed
where a clump of marigolds rocketed out

of the soil into tiny parachutes floating
into relocation. We scattered like dice
in a Yahtzee game and fled out the side door,

the back door, behind the dumpster
or into the Pizza Hut. One brave teen
locked the front door and left the woman

alone in the parking lot, glaring. Another
shouted, *We've called the police,* but the woman
aimed her baretta at the sky and scoffed,

Shouldn't've called the police. It'll only take us
longer. She shuffled towards her truck and shot
another batch of marigolds trembling through sky

just as the police sprang from their cars
and cuffed her from behind. *I'm not the one you*
should be arresting, she said. *I haven't held anyone up.*

CAITLIN JOHNSON

It Had to Be Done

It was inauspicious from the start.
We angels were unparalleled
& we were equal,
until someone—YOU KNOW WHO—
decided to play favorites.

He should have known.
He's the one who gave me this disposition.

Funny word, isn't it?
So close to dispossession—
the way he pushed the others out
to put me at his right hand.

But I believe in the collective:
the power, the glory
of all.

& that's why I had to leave him.
He threatened the others by loving me.
He forgot their value & their excellence.

So maybe I was a little violent when I went.
But I'm nothing if not flamboyant
(get it? FLAMboyant?),
& frankly, it was worth it to restore order.

Please Allow Me

Vol

u

bil

i

ty

Noun:

the possibility of turning

until you reach something,

or nothing at all,

as on a spit.

& mine, the hand that twists.

Mu

Home.
Crisscrossing water like veins:
& when it's fresh, you feel pure.

Away.
Absent freshwater,
salt everywhere & toxic.

GREG FIELD

Getting Warm…

Let us speak of God
as if he were a nightmare.
Let us be awed by his
nothingness as if he
were a shallow shadow
so that when we stand
in that gray light we feel
our stomachs turn
and we step out and away.
If we see the others,
we will push each one
into the shadow where
they grow ill and stumble
into the shadow's sides as if
they'd been eaten by a ghost.
They will kneel and pray
together like a broken heart
wailing their common doom.
We can take satisfaction
in their dead stares as
the shadow grows darker
and contracts to a
tiny black hole surrounded
by flame, and we can take
satisfaction in the heat of
our bright burning lives.

Fingers

Sometimes the corner
of his eye will sting
and he'll suddenly
reach up and rub
the skin at the edge
of its socket surprised
how random the world
can be, how random
his body with all
its surfaces, nooks
and crannies can
thwart his attempts
at silence as he sits
on his plastic chair
sipping his yard beer.
Forget contemplation
he thinks. To hell
with a chance at even
a tiny distance from
the world where a leaf
and a branch trouble
his hair. The world
has come to bear on
the corner of his eye
and that sting grows
into a terrible pain
that expands with each
stroke of his dry, split
fingers.

Three Rules for Dying

First, you must actually die.
With a blade, slice through
your life, paper soul, over-
written and dark with words
of senseless attempts at love—
a whole world described
by the spittle of a kiss.

Second, you must actually lose
your clothes—the cotton gown
flapping from your arms,
attendants huffing in the halls
calling your name—at last
you are famous among those
who will never know you.

Third, you must slip from the air
shedding your lungs and
tiny inert heart and the stained sheet
of someone's promised forgiveness.
Your soul, now naked and clean—
you must sink up into the stars
where you've spent most of
your life naked and dreaming.

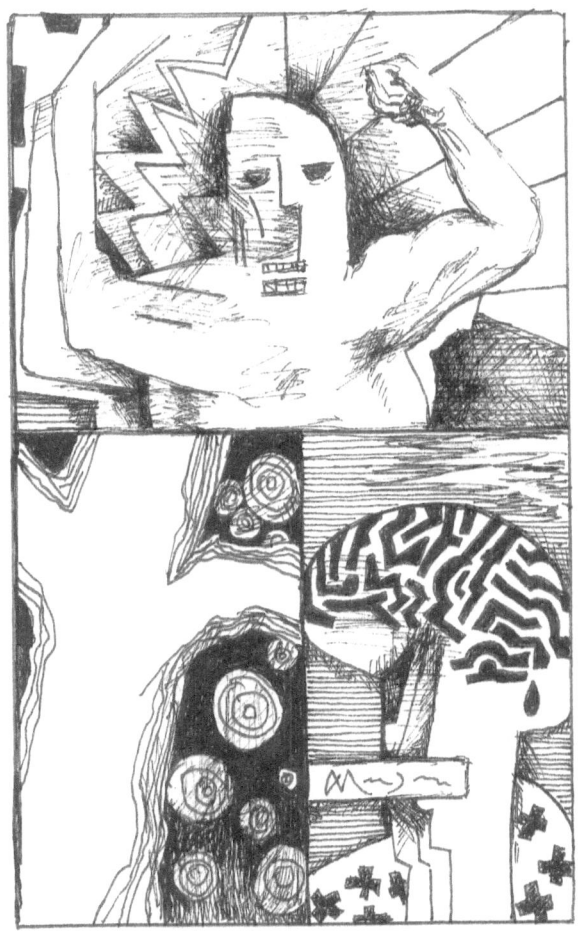

pentel pen 11x17cms 3-3-22, by Normon J. Olson

EVE RIFKAH

Change of address – 3rd birch from the trail

She didn't want it to be this way
thought growing up had possibilities
even with crazy ma and gone pa
whoever he was

In the dream she wakes in a warm room
sunlight rivering the floor
a cat stretched out mid-stream
in the dream the scent of coffee
twirls her awake

Instead, cold bites her nose
the old sleeping bag not up to low temps
the tent sags under roof of snow
knows she must move, to get going
find some warmth
pulls her clothes from the foot of the bag
struggles to dress without emerging
pulls on another sweater
layers to keep warm or fool herself
into warm

Stumbles down the hill
branches reach for her
want holding her back
she pulls herself together

catches the bus – free now – thankfully
as she fingers coins in her pocket

A meeting with a counselor
another faint hope
or false one
more trying to call numbers to nowhere
rings without end, to what the hell

She remembers the wish to be adopted
to have a family, birthday gifts,
a full stomach
the gypsies let her down
didn't come to search her out

Beautification, the Green Street Bridge

Not Here
here being the railway bridge over Green St.
here being the main drag from downtown
to the new ballpark – don't want folks
to be offended or scared   oh no

we being those with nice homes
those who want to believe
their city untainted

one of the board of selectmen
offered a suggestion
put up colored flashing lights
call it Art

beautifying the neighborhood
while making sure those dirty homeless
won't sleep there anymore
make the lights flash fast
make it unwelcoming for sleep

but oh, pretty colors
to walk through ---- quickly
on the way to a game.

the street people swept from one

place to another so much trash.

clean city what we need

clean of refuse of the unwanted

the used up   the lost

Chowder

A day of snow – no place to go – the plows making their hourly runs.
at the market cod on sale thick filets of white fish
add in sweet potatoes since no white ones left
carrots tiny diced, onions and garlic.
the chowder scent - dill and thyme – floats through the house.

I heard tell, one could walk across the harbor
on the backs of cod so plentiful they were.
now humans devouring the land breed faster than fish.
we will eat the earth clean and dry.
turn to each other with hunger in our eyes.

Today I make chowder as wind whips around corners
crying of times ahead, portents of dark.
time unravels   clocks spin in reverse
a golden-haired child runs through peripheral vision
there but not there
memory can't catch the fleeting boy
now grown and gone.

Running Dogs In The Ozarks

Clint swears he heard the sun sing.
A great big golden voice
pushed through the thinning leaves,
autumn's final defenders moved to dance.
Even the sky knows its master,
the foliage, too. It bowed
with the wind that morning,
clearing the way for clamor, the joyful noise
of natural order, foothill traditions.
Dogs barked. Snap-twig war drums
kept time with the gunfire.
The killing was done, but the music continued.
They cut the beasts open and kept shooting.
Three blasts for each of God's blessings,
hollers heard well into the night.

Murieta

For men who followed
gold veins into Earth's brittle chest,
chipped away at its core,
its grand cytoplasm of stone and decay,
they sure find their moments
to flounder and rot like beasts.

The thoughtless collapse
of decency.

A pistol glints in the sun.
Light for once,
the warm hand of morning,
an assurance that beginnings
always come at the end of darkness.

Revenge is like freshly cured ham.
It stings the tongue.
Salt and sugar, the way
fat and flesh melt
into sweet sensation.

Justice is like dynamite.
A fuse trimmed too short,
blows up at the wrong time,
hurts the wrong people.

Annie Oakley

"There is nothing more dangerous than a woman with a shotgun…"
-Louis L'amour

She barked about gentle movement.

Finesse and wonder, rode in wild loops.

Heaven's adulation, crowds tend to mimic thunder.

Golden girl of the sagebrush.

Felt, leather, and silk.

Wise gifts at future's window.

Short speeches on fame's blissful presence.

How opportunity is a moving target.

Why it's important to keep your guns clean.

Crosshatching

after Maurice Sendak

Close your eyes / Have no fear
The monster's gone / He's on the run
and your daddy's here

from "Beautiful Boy" by John Lennon

How long I've been waiting to grow
out of so many jimmy-rigged somethings,
the weight of words, the dread that chafes,
narrow escapes from stews and stagnancies—
from heavy sets of thoughts
from the full load of who we are
from my mother's 1940 crimson copy
of The Story of a Hundred Operas
tiny and tattered deep in my bedside bookcase.

Imagination could stretch in these caves,
organize our world with flirty wonderhorn
our pockets brimming with tiny bells
our cloaks of tender cascades, folds upon folds.
O Wild, O Goose-step
 O Dark Delectable,
O Right of Rain.
And you the accordion, Beautiful Boy
top-heavy & heavy-footed
with melodies that wickedly rhyme.
Please help me solve this poem.

My hand turns to overleaf—
your bare heels teasing piano keys
your Ragged Andy with inked heart,
your sock monkey with just one button eye,
the hubbub, the rumpus, the gaga
of you flying with fingernail wings
searching for the afikomen
in clefts & chasms—yet
memories no longer recognize you,
your dark clouds arming events.

Could we drop our plumb lines right into the heart of it
on the other side of moon
with incantatory words, embroider our story
puffs of dust under our running feet
the wagging tails of dreams
the lair of reveries for connective tissue,
inside with outside, outside with inside,
the wonder in rolling with surgical precision
a boiled egg beneath a knife blade
to release whole
its smooth and ready yolk.

You Were Here

for Uncle Lenny

The comfort in diorama,
the heft in my hands.
Your thigh high boots, fringed purses,
nightgowns cotton & girly.
Gloopy fables off kilter,
captions in lipstick red.
Your timeline
never straight but loopy.
Your mossy stones lovesick
with pillowy coats
of rococo frosting.
Cosmic stews with
grit washed away
to pump up the kernels,
skies of smoked orange,
acorn thrones for pixies.
Water balloons
& flour bombs,
elegance of updo,
flashing nipples, the fluff
of your abundant,
double-barreled.
So full of zoom.
Everything beamed at you,
   brightly sour,
      minced sweet.

Effing

Effing what we mean to say. Effing what we say is mean.
Effing twittering beats and pundit teats into
every night's howling. Effing to-do lists
with no to-don't lists. Effing parades of melodrama,
with so many first-person pronouns licking their navels.
Effing refrains and refrains of twerking and hollow
ta-dah-ing. Effing no one skips or whistles
anymore except maybe some children. Effing
doomsdays lurking under rugs swept there
by coward politicians. Effing all these effings
and my two clenched fists,
trigger fingers stuck and locked
into effing.

LISA BROGNANO

Upstream of Kwena Dam

Distant thunder growled in dictation
to a mask of clouds,
puncturing a still evening grayed by close rain;

the deep throat of un-hush-able booms
came in comfort to those
below, friends of the Zulus. Its waterfall tongue—

sourced from the winding Crocodile
River—commanded a flow
to dampen all things. Proper balance of a sapless

world pooled Mopani worms in grasses
as night fell slickly on
flowering places, crops roasted by dry spells,

partly shaded by Buffalo Thorn. Clay pots
overflowed near bush beans
and eggfruit, a wind pump mashing the downpour

against its paddles, chastising it for the delay,
          the want of a flooded sky
to pass down mist and herbs and nectar sooner

Wall Streeters & the Gin-Drinking
Apple-Knocker

Meant to be properly toothed off the skewer
and not bobbed like drowning rats, pickled
onions in a Gibson martini were being shame-

fully abused by a man under moonlight on
the deck; she saw him touch the tempered
glass railing with cucumber tea wedges

in a plate on the ledge—assuring he, nor
anyone else, would plummet into the middle
of lower Manhattan . . .

To dip silverskins in gin and vermouth
suggested to her, the recipient of an oriental
medicine degree, with a focus on herbology

and the synthesis of curative practices, that
all parties with a view of the East River
were not created equal. She would, however,

introduce herself, attempt to modify
his behavior, and glean how he knew Finn,
her Wall Street brother, who usually

preferred non-eccentric types in guests . . .
Perhaps folks in the financial market, savvy
by day, redirected their energies by night

Excusing her way through the crowd
should be worth hearing what a voice thick
with martini onions would sound like

in warm, musky air, with twenty other guests
chatting by the rail, fingering fungus cups
of ripe pear, sprinkled with cardamom—

what Finn called exotic pairings that
impressed women; but she took the selection
of someone to talk to as if under oath, in case

rambling on about western medicine's
pitfalls—its deprivation to the soul—were less
well received by a total stranger at Finn's

Indian Animal Fables, 200 BCE

I. Growing Season:

High Summer 2020

Aiming an old garden hose at a brush rabbit
spared her vegetables a sharp-tooth gnawing.
More expressly, the chipmunk burrow, corked
with a large rock, rerouted hazelnuts to another
larder, or would do so come High Fall. Four-
legged nuisances shimmied under

> the fence at the property line
> to destroy what she'd built

II.Elephants and Hares:

Panchatantra Tales

Surrounded by a pleasant source of water,
the hares enjoyed living conditions with little
care, letting leverets roam and play

But one day, a large herd of elephants invaded,
their journey forced by a dried-up pond. With
mighty stomps, they destroyed dark chambers
built around the water, killing many. The hares
feared the worst, comparing themselves to the
tuskers, but an idea led to a strategy,

> a way to make the trespassers
> flee in haste and never return

III. Moon God:

from the Sanskrit

Before leading the Elephant King to the water,
the hare described the Moon God's anger over
this disruption to the lake and hares he protects.
The king, in order to depart, wished to ask
forgiveness, and was shown the white reflection
in the water, being told the furious god

> had descended to console
> them over their great loss

IV. David and Goliath:

the God of Israel

Rock, sling, and faith knocked the giant down,
as everyone knew, but the hare wove a moon tale,
making a bright, stunning satellite a god over the
lumbering elephants, their feet broad like burrow
chambers, their spirits unnerved by a deity they'd
angered. Never to slurp from the reservoir again,

> the herd pushed on—hares
> protected by a pale moon

BENJAMIN KUZEMKA

1

Dmitriva help me, I've fallen in love with a story
of dusk and Dr Pepper, online shopping,
destruction, and bloodless rebirth.

You should see the screens and the packages;
you should see the Amazon trucks lost in the snow.

I've been to America and it smells of buttered
popcorn and burning CD's.
You should inhale the waxes with me.

Sit, or at least kindly ask me to.
Offer the localist of drinks,
the tenderest of apples.

You believe in silence, and I don't because I've seen
good men martyred by the saints.
But I know you believe in silence,
and I know you are correct.

Please cough for me twice, babushka.
Squeeze this hand like you used to and
take and burn my mandolin and pummel me with stories.
I've been to America.
It's more than me but less than you.
It is what we by accident choose.

2

Out of something you will form
and emerge, asleep as I pant
asleep as we scrub floors and hands
and pantries and play Liszt on low.

You are no longer dust.
I think of your pebble eyes
closed into my pebble arms.

Man, I'm just a rich kid with a guitar.
I can give you light but nothing more.

And neither can the saints
who will one day come
to take you away, away to Argentina
where I once buried flowers
on a mountainside and asked
the dusk to stop shaking.

It is not your turn to forgive me, not yet.
But when that late afternoon comes,
please call me by my name,
which is yours to remake. And do.

3

I have been struck by something
my phone calls 'Havana Syndrome.'

I rise early each morning
angry and slow reaching down
and taking the good names in vain.

I cough when I walk, sigh where I sit,
whiff hummus to make sure I can still smell.
I think of basketball and the comments
I'll soon write about it.

I price everything out, vision boarding well
next September when there might
be more tulips in bloom.

In India a street vendor
once told me that I looked like
Saint Paul, himself.

Well, I smiled and still do,
only from the side.

JEFF WEDDELL

Manifesto

Who do we write for, if not the people?
The professors and preachers and bosses
don't want or need us.
They are filled with the dogma of the ages.
What use would they have for poetry?
Ask the professors and they will say
they know what poetry is, what it is not
and who is allowed to write it. Fuck them.
Ask the preachers and they will say
the hateful verse of two thousand years
past is plenty to keep us all sated, tithing,
frightened and in line. Fuck them.
Ask the bosses and they will say
they know nothing of poetry
and want to keep it like that
for themselves and also for their workers.
Small minds like small minds and,
even more, the pursuit of money. Fuck them.
But the workers, some of them,
need what we offer,
even if they do not know it.
The same is true for the destitute,
the forgotten, the thrown away.
It is true for young people not yet calcified

by routine and lies.

It is true for the free of spirit,

the seekers, the sad, the lonely, the bright,

the odd, the skulkers in the dark,

the exuberant, the paranoid, the sex fiends,

the drug fiends, the drunks, the mad

and the joyful.

It is true for our beleaguered planet,

being killed minute by minute

by the mindless replication of yesterday.

The people need poetry

even if they do not know it.

Stick to your task, brothers and sisters.

Write new dreams and visions.

This is the balm we bring.

This is what holds the light of the world.

Driving the Lost Highway

In the car with my poems
hiding somewhere under the seat
or maybe in the glove compartment.
I watch the beautiful sky and say, firmly,
that I wish my poems were here
to see it with me,
hoping to shame them
into not being coy
and share their company. No dice.
I see an old lady who looks like a prophet
out of the Old Testament
and know my poems would love her,
but I don't even try,
because I'm mad at them
and they don't deserve to see her.
Well, more hurt than mad. But still.
I'm in the car with my poems somewhere
and heading down a highway most people
never knew and most others have forgotten.
It's near sunset and the sky is a dying grey,
but huge and beautiful.
Strong clouds, majestic birds,
eagles and hawks,
a steady wind.
No more people around and the old lady
has gone somewhere she's supposed to,

a pipeline to the mysteries.

I stop trying to lure out my poems

and settle into the drive.

I roll down the windows. I crank the radio.

I sing as loud as I can.

That's when the poems finally come out.

I say hello to them.

They say hello right back.

We sing together as the sun goes down,

off key and glorious.

The stars appear and we sing right out loud.

At Your Service

The washing of the feet
as annoyed goats bite at the legs
of drunk shepherds
who have mistaken them for sheep.
The glories and the hallelujahs. The horny
housewives
eyeing the horny high school jocks
as the preacher goes on and on.
There are stars. Someplace.
I am certain of it.
Maybe out past the moon.
Way out there in the dark.
The goats sing the highest psalms
in their goat language. (Syntax is problematic.
They are goats, after all.)
The blood on their teeth
embarrasses entire congregation.
The young girls in their new bodies
mouth words to awful hymns
and glow the way they do.
One of them might kill someone
before the day is over,
but never mind.
I have said too much
already.

MARK HENNESSY

Love Poem On A Liquor Store Sack

Let's begin w/ the labials: you like yer name again? I
never stopped: & how many nights did I torture myself
w/ indecent thoughts of you my Betty Page Cattle Baron
ess? Stumble into your sanctuary to have my raging app
etites becalmed & fussed over? Do you remember the train
brakeairhorns of the rapture like I do? How I woke up shive
ring like a junkie from yer clawfoot immaculate tub to the
gentle tracing of yer fingertips against the inside of my
elbows? & how yer sorrow reflected my own: oh river
to carve a cliff with, oh unforgettable cursive slant, what
songs you played on yer piano, sound melody made per
fect, Sarah Cole's Love Story, & Borges read aloud &
how I fell in love w/ you again just passing yer old back
door. Still hard to do good hard mama. & who carried
that piano up those stairs? They must have loved you or
been well paid, & where, when we did stop on the high
way outta town, was it cuz the rye ran out? Or my despair
caught up? Haunt me again outside my brother's trailer:
we can dance again for hours inside the bathroom turned
dance floor. Jesus Christ protect us, save us all from get
ting what we wish for—save me from the abandon w/
which you dance w/ me tonight. Or if not that—then
please oh please, from the days to follow w/o it—

Calm Seas Never Made A Skilled Sailor: Days w/o Incident: 0

Here's to all the stupid old shit—like mailing a
letter. I kept the arcade photo strip outtov it/
did not draw the cloud of the day on the env
elope, tho there is a kite inside, & but I sent it
just the same. & that is my kindov masochism:
sharp needle dangling on the red thread inside
my jacket, roaring tiger w/o. Burned the last
letter I sent the day she got it & it did make a
lovely flame—I wrote her I hope I am not stu
pid to feel this way when I know I am so so s
tupid to feel this way—maybe the bacteria in
my gut wants, so proud of our grinning scar,
like cigarettes extinguished on the pale skin of
our hip, want this pain, our favorite, to remain.
She took my ex-wife's call only to confirm my
death, asked me to text to ignore my messages.
demanded to be put on my docket, inquired as to
my travel plans: winked to see if I'd jump & I sed
how high? We were perfect for one another. Just
were. Yes, better together. But bro/ken apart. & so
we became perfect at breaking. Better judges of dis
tance now. I laid bare my idiocy admirably, why
not buy all in, bury myself up to my neck in my
misery, allow the frailest part of me to drown in
all the breath-taking heartache full consideration
of her loss brings, so sad: she's the one that died,

the myth of true love abandoned, betrayed, for a
gasping absence—& all the sheet lightning in the
summer Kansas sky illuminating my hidden fingers,
her wanton mouth, will not discharge a mote of
the ache of it. Look: All our love poems & love songs:
just more paperwork–

Love Song for Global Warming

Oh heat! How, how kind you are to me
inside & out: I have it on good authority
there are those who'd view the tsunami
dead as god's justly punished—but I can't
buy that: no island sins all the same: e.g.
I'm pretty sure we're breaking at least
three laws, maybe more since the state
we're in, in my mini-eden golf-cart but
tucked into the tall pine & outta site
from squares behind the boatshelf: are
we sinning? Like our sun I radiate heat
& the heat sez no, sez sin if so harder &
faster: recited some John Milton Satan
in the Provision Fish Co. & now they let
me grab my own beers from the kitchen
cooler—& there's a lesson there about
me, about sin, about heat, wilting illegible
& instructing us damned to sing as we speak—

KRISTIN J. THOMPSON

Cassette tape of a phantom who hasn't been born yet

I raised up in a stolen town dirtied by coal and oil,
bones abandoned in the driveway, and peanuts in my pocket.
Labs and Frenchies circled tails
while fleas ricocheted meals between fur and eyelids,
a bacchanal hosted on the country of our dermis.

Root beer and icebox hinges financed the superiority complexes,
one man's relish and ragged jeans are
another man's objective,
Narcan is stored in every hairspray headmistress's
medicine cabinet, because the potluck was canceled and
the daughter is dead.

One morning, I woke up and wasn't small anymore
but I still felt like it.
A draft escorted a cigarette to my doorstep,
an invisible portal calloused by the tar of teen boys and their
excuses.
I am 16, riding shotgun in a blue mustang to a rich man's palace
when I am really in love with the penniless poet.

I wrote him letters down by the Quercus Palustris,
camouflaging my affections with pine needles and bandages,
traipsing through crawdads and wildflower arrangements

until arriving at the house where no one lived,
except maybe the spirits.

The belching oven sprawled open, and out
came a phantogram of church sermons,
all screaming with gaping mouths
in silent unison
"Deliverance, Deliverance!"

A collapsed bathroom wall is wheat-floured to
yellow paper that weather nor fire could resist befriending.
Green stalks of flora are woven delicately into the asbestos,
the color of wild onions, courageously sprouting as though
they were always there to begin with.

I am fingering the pulse of something that has departed,
somewhere between the soul and the tendons,
the musical-chair indisposition of the wounded dog
and the car that hit him.
You must understand,
this was always going to happen.
And the wild onion will continue to sprout
through cracks in concrete
no matter the season.

Joe's Cafe

A letter to Polly

Polly,

you were 7 carpeted stairs directly above my head

while I was attempting to convince

a brute in overalls to love me.

Not even Jazz could have consoled me.

However, in hindsight, if Satan was playing the sax that night

I would have dropped that seashell pink halter frock

and fucked him in front of the entire assembly

than to have allowed this riddle of a man to recapture me.

Polly,

you witnessed the end of an era

without even realizing that you were looking.

That night I felt things, funny enough,

only God might understand,

like the affliction of when a man who hates you

makes you cum

and you recommence with a swollen tongue because

you're already infected.

Polly,

this is my version of Armageddon:

each of my personalities gathering

at a claustrophobia-inducing music venue

lit by nothing but ash and a neon "Radio" sign,

all battling to conquer the bathroom line
which leads to nothing but the pelvis
of a man seeking refuge in the mirror.

Polly,
You were drinking a BYOB extra dry martini
and were too busy roaring and falling in love
to notice my epiphany as I emerged from the space-time continuum.
There was no man,
there was only me and the fallen goblin
and I surely did fuck him.

The Purple House

for Mackenzie

Two red roses bloom out of a mug that reads "Mackinac Island".
My grandmother would have loved you.
Our cars in the driveway are swimming in mud and pollen
as we mingle in cool air writing a song about a garden.
While we sing, a rabbit rots on concrete in quiet desiccation.
I wait until you leave to bury it.
Though I am attached to its innocence,
I want to spare you the burden.
Dragonflies are painted and peeling off the house
which symbolizes an eternal spring,
like a lonely opus created by someone with a terminal god complex.
Two golden keys hang from a nail in the kitchen.
I dance and sing to Nina Simone
while baking pasta in a casserole dish.
You come home and kiss me on the forehead
while shower steam rises in grapefruit and jasmine opulence.

Where did I love you?
Between the pickle brine and the pesto
Between the old rag and the mirror
Between two wooden chairs and a blue bottle
Between a spider and a washing machine
Between an empty bedroom and a wish?
I knew I loved you from our first kiss.

A bouquet rests on my pillow.

My body is available to you in ways that

She has never been.

The sun shines on our faces until we burn

Until we are forced to jump into the river,

Until the sun goes down again.

A porch swing sways in a smoke haze from your last cigarette.

I'm sorry that I asked you to quit.

I just couldn't imagine my life without you in it.

ADRIAN LIME

A Stabbing

Walking home from work
late night in despair back to South Toledo,
those lonely late night thoughts of leaving,
of got to get out, go somewhere—
just go and go somewhere else—

a thin figure runs up to me from warehouse side-street
out of the dark, shouts *Gimme your fuckin money man*

He looks like he's 13 years old
nervous. Licking his lips—
pokes my side with a stick blade
then runs away with nothing.

I had nothing to give him, anyway.
I lift my shirt and look down
more surprised, than in pain

and watch the blood roll out of me
like a fast train leaving a lonely station.

My Father's Grave

My father's gravestone is newer
than the stone path that wanders
through these aged trees and fields of graves
of mothers and uncles, loving children
and each sort of dearest departed.

My father's gravestone— too new
to be rounded by wind and rain
and freeze of seasons,
memories sharp enough to cut
hands that would hold it.

Unwilling to bend to the swell
of the soft earth around it
my father's grave wants cold ground
wants frozen ground.

Poem for My Son

I want to tell you
we will always be happy

that shadows are
just flat, empty things
silly to fear

but sometimes
there are things in the shadows
that wish us harm

sometimes, no matter how we try,
they follow us into the light
out into the open
the safe places

sometimes they will find your heart
and hold tight, squeeze hard
until you finally give in
or outlast them

outlast them

The Players:

Jeff Alfier's most recent book, *The Shadow Field*, was published by Louisiana Literature Press (2020). Journal credits include *Carolina Quarterly, CopperNickel, The Emerson Review, Faultline, Hotel Amerika, New York Quarterly, Penn Review, Southern Poetry Review,* and *Vassar Review.*

M.J. Arcangelini, born in Pennsylvania in 1952, has resided in northern California since 1979. He has published in little magazines, online journals (including *The James White Review, Rusty Truck, The Ekphrastic Review, Trailer Park Quarterly, As It Ought To Be Magazine, The Rye Whisky Review,* and *Live Nude Poems*), & over a dozen anthologies. He is the author of 6 published collections, the most recent of which is *PAWNING MY SINS,* 2022 (Luchador Press).

Tohm Bakelas is a social worker in a psychiatric hospital. He was born in New Jersey, resides there, and will die there. His poems have appeared in numerous journals, zines, and online publications. He is the author of 13 chapbooks, one full length book of poetry, and his work has been nominated several times for the Pushcart Prize. He runs Between Shadows Press.

Jonathan S Baker lives all alone by the frowning river. They are the author of *Long Nights in Stoplight City* (Between the Shadows Press, 2023) and *Thump! Thump!* (Laughing Ronin Press, 2023). They are also co-editor at *The Grind Stone.*

James Benger has written a bunch of stuff. Some of it has even been published in print and on the interwebs. So far there are two ebooks, three chapbooks, six splits, and two full-lengths. He is the resident slacker on the Board of Directors of the Writers Place, and is the most truant member of the Riverfront Readings Committee. He is also the admin of an online poetry workshop called 365 Poems in 365 Days. He lives and Kansas City with his wife and children.

Dianne Borsenik is active in the northern and mid-Ohio poetry communities. Recent work appears in *I Thought I Heard a Cardinal Sing: Ohio's Appalachian Voices, Birds of the Cuyahoga,* and *Slipstream.* Lit Youngstown printed her poem "Disco" on their tee shirts, which makes her feel like a rock star.

Maria Vasquez Boyd is producer/host, of Artspeak Radio a weekly live program on 90.1FM KKFI Kansas City Community Radio. Since 2012, she features local and world renowned artists, writers, poets, playwrights locally and internationally. Boyd is a founding member of the Latino Writers Collective, a storyteller, poet, artist, designer, painter, and continues to exhibit her work across the country. She served as Poet in Residence for Present Magazine in Kansas City, Missouri.

Lisa Brognano is the author of the novels *In the Interest of Faye* (Golden Antelope, 2017) and *A Man for Prue* (Resplendence, 2017). Her full-length poetry books include: *The Willow Howl* (Nixes Mate, 2017), The Copper Weathervane (Luchador, 2020), and Royal Blue Shutters (Fernwood Press, 2022). Her poems and short fiction have appeared in national and international literary journals. In December 2021, her latest manuscript was shortlisted for the Sexton Poetry Prize. Brognano holds a master's degree in English and another in Fine Art. She lives in New York with her husband.

Tony Brewer is from Bloomington, Indiana. His latest books are *Pity for Sale* (Gasconade Press, 2022) and *psithurism* (Last Lights Press, 2022). He is also a frequent collaborator with experimental music collective Urban Deer. More at tonybrewer71.blogspot.com.

Kristofer Collins is the publisher of Low Ghost Press and the books editor at *Pittsburgh Magazine.* He is the co-host of the Hemingway's Summer Poetry Series. He is the author of *The River Is Another Kind of Prayer: New & Selected Poems* and *Roundabout Trace* both published by Kung Fu Treachery. He lives in Pittsburgh, PA with his wife Dr. Anna Johnson and their children Cassidy and Joni.

\

Diane Vogel-Ferri is a teacher, poet, and writer living in Solon, Ohio. Her latest novel is *No Life But This: A Novel of Emily Warren Roebling*. Her essays have been published in *Scene Magazine, Yellow Arrow Journal, Cleveland Christmas Memories, Good Works Review,* and by Cleveland State University among others. Her poems can be found in numerous journals such as *Wend Poetry, Rubbertop Review, American Journal of Poetry,* and *Poet Lore*. Her previous publications are: *Liquid Rubies* (poetry), *The Volume of Our Incongruity* (poetry), and *The Desire Path* (novel). Diane's essay, "I Will Sing for You" was featured at the Cleveland Humanities Festival in 2018.

Steve Gerson, an emeritus English professor from Johnson County Community College, writes poetry and flash about life's dissonance and dynamism. He's proud to have been named a finalist for the 2021 Poetry of the Plains & Prairies (POPP) Award. Steve has published in *Panoplyzine* (winning an Editor's Choice award), *Hungry Chimera, Toe Good, Write Launch, Route 7, Duck Lake, Coffin Bell, Poets Reading the News, Crack the Spine, White Wall Review, Variant, Abstract, Montana Mouthful, Decadent Review, Indolent, Rainbow Poems, Snapdragon, Underwood Press, Wingless Dreamer, Gemini Ink, Dillydoun Review, Elevation Review, Poet's Choice, Lucky Jefferson, Novus Literary, In Parentheses, South Florida Poetry Journal, 86 Logic, Two Timbers,* and *Constellations*.

Ken Gierke is a retired truck driver, transplanted to Missouri from Western New York. After only ten years here, he is actually coming to think of Missouri as home, in spite of muddy water and a dearth of maple trees. While his poetry has appeared in several anthologies, this is his first published collection.

Tony Gloeggler was born and raised in New York City. He is theauthor of several full-length poetry collections, including *What Kind Of Man* 2020, *The Last Lie* (2010), *One Wish Left* (2002). His chapbook *One on One* won the 1998 Pearl Poetry Prize.

Westley Heine is the author of *Busking Blues: Recollections of a Chicago Street Musician and Squatter, 12 Chicago Cabbies,* and *The Trail of Quetzalcoatl.* His poetry and prose have been published in *The Chicago Reader, Gravitas, Heroin Love Songs, Beatdom, Dumpster Fire Press,* and *The Wellington Street Review* among others. He's been a taxi dispatcher, a roadie, a deliveryman, a squatter, a street musician, a grocery clerk, a chambermaid, a novelist, a painter, a metal head, a Boy Scout, an insurance investigator, a jailbird, a farmhand, sold tickets to the symphony, sold plasma, been unemployed, and been a filmmaker. Life is always creating new characters inside him, but always a writer. Originally from Wisconsin he's rambled to Europe, Mexico, California, and everywhere in between. He now resides in Chicago. Let in the light. Let out the fire. Instagram: @westleyheine

Mark Hennessy walked the Earth long before we were here and will walk the Earth long after we are gone.

Caitlin Johnson is the author of three chapbooks and two full-length poetry collections, including *Delta* from Stubborn Mule Press. Her work has appeared in *Pembroke Magazine, Vagina: The Zine, Slippery Elm Literary Journal,* and many others. She lives in Michigan.

Mike Jurkovic A 2016 Pushcart nominee, Mike's poetry and music reviews have been published globally but with little reportable income. Full length collections include *mooncussers,* (Luchador Press 2022); *AmericanMental,* (Luchador Press 2020). *Blue Fan Whirring* (Nirala Press, 2018) Anthologies: *Calling All Poets 20th Anniversary Anthology,* (CAPS Press); *Reflecting Pool: Poets & the Creative Process* (Codhill Press, 2018); *Like Light: 25 Years of Poetry & Prose* (Bright Hill Press, 2018) among others. Now in its 23rd year, he serves as President of Calling All Poets. CD reviews online at All About Jazz and Lightwood. Mike serves as chairman of the curated Music Fan Series, Rosendale Theater. He hosts New Jazz Excursions alternating Saturdays 10am-12pm on WIOX 91.3FM, Roxbury, NY. Streaming live at wioxradio.org. *The Rock n Roll Curmudgeon* appeared in Rhythm and News Magazine, 1996-2003. He loves Emily most of all.

Paul Koniecki lives and writes in Dallas, Texas. He was once chosen for the John Ashbery Home School Residency. His poems feature in Richard Bailey's movie "One of the Rough" distributed by AVIFF Cannes. His previous books are available from Kleft Jaw Press, NightBallet Press, Dark Particle Press, Spartan Press, and Between Shadows Press. Paul proudly sits on the editorial board of *Thimble Literary Magazine*. His poems have appeared in *ENTROPY, Gasconade Review, As It Ought To Be Magazine, River Dog, Blue Max Review, Chantarelle's Notebook,* and many more.

Benjamin Kuzemka grew up in suburban Chicago and now lives in suburban St. Louis with his spouse and two young children. He has one published collection of poetry, *Dance Grooves for Gotikara* (Spartan Press, 2018), and his work has appeared in *Gasconade Review, U City Review,* and *Montage Arts Journal.*

Dawne Leiker is a native of western Kansas. She is the author of two collections of poetry, including *Death of the Civic Minded Man* (self-published) and *what remains* (Spartan Press, 2022).

Adrian Lime is a poet, spray paint artist, and UAW autoworker. A founding member of Toledo's Almeda Street Poets, he helped to launch the Toledo Poetry Museum and ToledoPoet.com. His books are *Feeding the Monster* (2018, EMP Books), a collaboration of factory poems with poet Michael Grover, and *Every Broken Little Thing* (2022, Luchador Press). Adrian works at the Toledo Jeep North Assembly plant, and lives in a nice little house in West Toledo with his wife.

Brenda Linkman began writing poetry when she was a sophomore in high school and only recently began publishing. She has had poems published in *The Gasconade Review* and the *Trailer Park Quarterly.* She has made a career working as a clinical social worker and play therapist with children, as well as teaching private art lessons. Brenda grew up moving frequently since her father was a topographic engineer for the USGS. She has lived in seventeen states. Living all over the U.S. allowed her to learn about the variety of landscapes in this country, and the often subtle, but unique cultural differences there are between the states. The dynamics between people inspires Brenda's poetry, as does the universe.

R. Nikolas Macioci earned a PhD from The Ohio State University, and for thirty years taught for the Columbus City Schools. In addition to English, he taught Drama and developed a Writers Seminar for select students. OCTELA, the Ohio Council of Teachers of English, named Nik Macioci the best secondary English teacher in the state of Ohio. Nik is the author of twelve books. Critics and judges called *Cafes of Childhood* a "beautifully harrowing account of child abuse," but not "sentimental" or "self-pitying," an "amazing book," and "a single unified whole." *Cafes of Childhood* was submitted for the Pulitzer Prize in 1992. In 2021, he was nominated for a Pushcart Prize and a Best of the Net award. In 2022, he was nominated for a Pushcart Prize. More than two hundred of his poems have been published here and abroad in magazines and journals, including *Chiron, Concho River Review, The Bombay Review, Humana Obscura,* and *West Trade Review.* He won First Place in the 1987 National Writer's Union Poetry Competition, judged by Denise Levertov, First Place in The Baudelaire Award Competition, sponsored by The World Orderof Narrative and Formalist Poets (1989), Second Place in Zone 3's first annual Rainmaker Awards, judged by Howard Nemerov (1989), and Second Place in the Writer's Digest annual competition, judged by Diane Wakoski (1991).

Poet, playwright and essayist **John Macker** grew up in Colorado and has lived in northern New Mexico for over 25 years. He has published 14 full-length books and chapbooks of poetry, 2 audio recordings, an anthology of fiction and essays, and several broadsides over 35 years. His most recent are *Belated Mornings, Atlas of Wolves, The Blues Drink Your Dreams Away, Selected Poems 1983-2018,* (a 2019 New Mexico-Arizona Book Awards finalist), *Desert Threnody,* essays and short fiction, (winner of the 2021 New Mexico-Arizona Book Awards fiction anthology prize) and *Chaco Sojourn,* short stories, (illustrated by Leon Loughridge and published in limited edition by Dry Creek Art Press.) For several years, he was contributor to Albuquerque's *Malpais Review.* His one-act play, "Coyote Acid" was produced by Teatro Paraguas in Santa Fe in early 2022. He lives in Santa Fe, on the El Camino Real, on ancestral Puebloan land, Gran Apacheria, with his wife Annie and two dogs.

Norman J. Olson is a small press poet and artist who lives in Maplewood, Minnesota

RC Patterson is a poet, lecturer. He is the author of eight books of poetry and prose, including *Black Lives Splatter* (2017, Bad Jacket Press), *Black Magic* (2018, Spartan Press), *Elegies* (2019), *House of Ganesha* (2022), *Act of Hericide* (2022), *You Need To Be Tougher* (2022), *Deinosology* (2022) and *The Necropolis of Abraxas* (2022). He also has work published in *Bad Jacket Magazine* and his poem "Untitled (2019, Stubborn Mule Press)" has been published in *After the Flood* by Greg Edmondson.

A poet and a father, **Kushal Poddar,** edited a magazine - *Words Surfacing,* and authored seven volumes of poetry including *The Circus Came To My Island, A Place For Your Ghost Animals, Eternity Restoration Project - Selected and New Poems* and *Herding My Thoughts To The Slaughterhouse - A Prequel.*

Kevin Ridgeway is the author of the poetry collections *Too Young to Know* (Stubborn Mule Press, 2019) and *Invasion of the Shadow People* (Luchador Press, 2022). His work has appeared in *The Paterson Literary Review, Slipstream, Chiron Review, Nerve Cowboy, Plainsongs, Spillway, Main Street Rag, The Cape Rock, San Pedro River Review, Meat for Tea, Trailer Park Quarterly, Misfit Magazine, Cultural Daily* and *The American Journal of Poetry,* among many others. A Pushcart Prize and Best of the Net nominee, he lives and writes in Long Beach, CA.

Eve Rifkah was co-founder of Poetry Oasis, Inc. (1998-2012), a non-profit poetry association dedicated to education and promoting local poets. Founder, and editor DINER, a literary magazine. She is the 2021 recipient of the Stanley Kunitz award. She has five published books. A play, *Outcasts the Lepers of Penikese Island*, based on her first book, *Outcasts the Penikese Island Leper Hospital*, 1905-1921, was performed at the American Academy of Dramatic Arts, NY. She lives in Worcester, MA. www.eve-rifkah.com

Linda Rocheleau is a veteran teacher, writer and poet living in Asheville, North Carolina. Recent publications include: *Trailer Park Quarterly*, *Savannah Literary Journal* and others.

Rikki Santer's poetry has received many honors including six Pushcart and three Ohioana and Ohio Poet book award nominations as well as a fellowship from the National Endowment for the Humanities. Her eleventh poetry collection, *Stopover*, which is in conversation with the original Twilight Zone series was recently published by Luchador Press. She is also a member of the teaching artist roster of the Ohio Arts Council, a vice president of the Ohio Poetry Association, and a member of the poetry troupe, Concrete Wink. Please contact her through her website: rikkisanter.com

Scott Silsbe was born in Detroit. He now lives in Wilkinsburg, Pennsylvania. His poems and prose have appeared in numerous periodicals and have been collected in the three books: *Unattended Fire, The River Underneath the City,* and *Muskrat Friday Dinner.* He is also an assistant editor at Low Ghost Press.

Christopher Stephen Soden received his MFA in Poetry from Vermont College of Fine Arts in January of 2005. He teaches craft, theory, genre and literature. He writes poetry, plays, literary, film and theatre critique for sharpcritic.com and Edge Dallas. Christopher's poetry collection, *Closer* was released by Rebel Satori Press on June 14th, 2011. He received a Full Fellowship to Lambda Literary's Retreat for Emerging LGBT Voices in August 2010. His performance piece: Queer Anarchy received The Dallas Voice's Award for Best Stage Performance. *Water* and *A Christmas Wish* were staged at Bishop Arts and Every Day is Christmas. In Heaven at Nouveau 47. Other honors include: Distinguished Poets of Dallas, Poetry Society of America's Poetry in Motion Series, Founding Member, President and President Emeritus of The Dallas Poets Community. His work has appeared in: *Rattle, The*

Cortland Review, 1111, Typishly, F(r)iction, G & L Review, Chelsea Station, Glitter- wolf, Collective Brightness, A Face to Meet the Faces, Resilience, Ganymede Poets: One, Gay City 2, The Café Review, The Texas Observer, Sentence, Borderlands, Off the Rocks, The James White Review, The New Writer, Velvet Mafia, Poetry Super Highway, Gertrude, Touch of Eros, Gents, Bad Boys and Barbarians, Windy City Times, ArLiJo, Best Texas Writing.

Carolyn Srygley-Moore (C Leigh Srygley aka) is a resident of Upstate New York with her husband and various animal rescues. She's a graduate of Johns Hopkins University where she won awards; has been privileged to study, via Albany's New York Writer's Institute, with the Irish poet John Montagu (RIP). She has worked with Real Stories Gallery, writing on various cultural pathologies like Trafficking. She has been published by I am not a silent poet, among many other journals; in the last 13 years has been nominated for 2 Pushcarts and one Best-of-the-Web. She's authored books and chapbooks, most notably *Ode to Horatio* and *Other Saviors* (Crisis Chronicles Press), *Miracles of the Blog;* a series (Punk Hostage Press) and *Termites amidst the Milky Way* (Kung Fu Treachery Press*).* No portions of this Book have been published elsewhere due to the nature of Putin's invasion of The Ukraine, the sense that the Book has just begun.

Timothy Tarkelly's work has appeared in *Ekstasis Magazine, Agape Review, Rhodora Magazine,* and others. He's authored several collections of poetry, including *Objects We Know We Don't Deserve: Poems on Dutch Art* (Alien Buddha Press), *Luckhound* (Spartan Press), and *Polling Data as a Means of Self-expression* (OAC Books). When he's not writing, he teaches in Southeast Kansas.

Kristin J. Thompson is a literary and visual artist currently living in St. Louis, Missouri. She is the author of 4 books of poetry and the co-founder of an indie literary press called Back of the Class Press. In her spare time, you can find her hosting film classes, creating tintypes, reading with her cat, raising moths, digging up bones over-seas, and curating art collectives. Her work can be viewed online at kristinjthompson.com.

Mack Thorn is a poet/artist from St. Louis, Missouri. He is the author of 3 collections of poetry, *The Black Paintings* (2019 Bad Jackett), *Fate of a Mullet* (2020 Spartan Press) and *Rattlesnakes and Flattops* (Impspired 2022). As well as two chapbooks *Strange Tales from Cherokee Street* (Spartan Press) and *The Great American Pyramid Scheme* (OAC Books 2022). His work can be found in literary journals such as 365 Days, Alien Buddha, Cajan Mutt Press, as well as online journals like *Rye Whiskey Review*. He is also a former resident artist at the Osage Arts Community. If he is not writing poetry or music, he can often be found eating chicken wings or collecting Jim Baker buckets.

Ohio born and raised, **Kerry Trautman** is a founder of ToledoPoet.com and the "Toledo Poetry Museum" page on Facebook, which promote Northwest Ohio poetry events. She was a poetry editor for *Red Fez* from 2016 until it closed in 2022. Her work has appeared in various anthologies and journals, and her books are *Things That Come in Boxes* (King Craft Press 2012,) *To Have Hoped* (Finishing Line Press 2015,) *Artifacts* (NightBallet Press 2017,) *To be Nonchalantly Alive* (Kelsay Books 2020,) and *Marilyn: Self- Portrait, Oil on Canvas* (Gutter Snob Books 2022.) and *Unknowable Things* (Roadside Press 2023.)

Agnes Vojta grew up in Germany and now lives in Rolla, Missouri where she teaches physics at Missouri S&T and hikes the Ozarks. She is the author of *Porous Land, The Eden of Perhaps,* and *A Coracle for Dreams,* all published by Spartan Press. Agnes is one of the nine poets who collaborated on the book *Wild Muse: Ozarks Nature Poetry* (Cornerpost Press, December 2022.) Her poems have appeared in a variety of magazines; you can read some of them on her websiteagnesvojta.com.

Maryfrances Wagner's newest books are *The Silence of Red Glass, The Immigrants' New Camera,* and *Solving for X*. Her newly reissued book *Red Silk* won the Thorpe Menn Book Award. She co-edits *I-70 Review,* serves on The Writers Place board, was 2020 Missouri Individual Artist of the Year, and is Missouri Poet Laureate 2021-2023. Poems have appeared in *New Letters, Midwest Quarterly, Laurel Review, American Journal of Poetry, Poetry East, Green Mountain Literary Review, Voices in Italian Americana, Main Street Rag, Rattle, Unsettling America: An Anthology of Contemporary Multicultural Poetry,* et. al. For more information, check her website: http://maryfranceswagnerwriter. fieldinfoserv.com/

Jeff Weddle is a poet and writer living in Tuscaloosa, Alabama. He won the Eudora Welty Prize for *Bohemian New Orleans: The Story of the Outsider* and Loujon Press, and has also received honors for his fiction and poetry. Jeff teaches in the School of Library and Information Studies at the University of Alabama.

ink 13x19cms 12-28-21, by Normon J. Olson

This project was made possible, in part, by generous support from the Osage Arts Community.

Osage Arts Community provides temporary time, space and support for the creation of new artistic works in a retreat format, serving creative people of all kinds — visual artists, composers, poets, fiction and nonfiction writers. Located on a 152-acre farm in an isolated rural mountainside setting in Central Missouri and bordered by ¾ of a mile of the Gasconade River, OAC provides residencies to those working alone, as well as welcoming collaborative teams, offering living space and workspace in a country environment to emerging and mid-career artists. For more information, visit us at www.osageac.org

Osage Arts Community

www.ingramcontent.com/pod-product-compliance
Lightning Source LLC
Chambersburg PA
CBHW031508120626

46545CB00005B/1785